180 PRAYERS

— for a —

Woman of Confidence

Print ISBN 978-1-64352-865-6

Published by Barbour Publishing, Inc., 1810 Barbour Drive, Uhrichsville, Ohio 44683, www.barbourbooks.com

Our mission is to inspire the world with the life-changing message of the Bible.

Member of the
Evangelical Christian
Publishers Association

180 PRAYERS

for a

Woman of Confidence

ELLIE ZUMBACH

BARBOUR
PUBLISHING

INTRODUCTION

When I thought about being confident, I always thought it was a strong belief in myself or my own choices. It was always self-focused and sometimes very self-centered. I take pride in how confident people say I am. But when I studied what Jesus had to say about confidence, I realized that if I'm only confident in myself and what I can do, I will always disappoint myself. So where can I go to get everlasting strength, power, and confidence?

The answer is always to God. If we develop a confidence from our heavenly Father, we access a well of strength that never dries up. It isn't distorted or damaged; we can be sure this confidence is the truth.

This book of prayers can be used for the moments when you can't find the words for what you're going through or feeling. It can be read straight through, or prayers can be read separately in no order at all. While God knows our hearts, He longs for conversation with us. Let these words be open doors to discussions with the Lord about how to become the confident woman He created you to be.

Much love,
Ellie

1

MADE IN HIS IMAGE

So God created mankind in his own image,
in the image of God he created them;
male and female he created them.
GENESIS 1:27 NIV

*L*ord, I know You created Eve with utmost care. She was the perfect pairing for Adam, crafted from his own body. But above this, Lord, I know Eve was formed in Your image. Before the Fall, Eve had no concept of beauty standards; she felt no inadequacy or unworthiness. All she knew was that she belonged to her Creator, and that was enough. It was only when sin entered the world that she became ashamed of herself. Ashamed of her body and her choices.

Father, I live in a world dominated by voices telling me what I should look like. It feels impossible to see myself the way You do—perfectly created for a purpose, made beautiful in the image of my Savior. Help me to be confident in the body You made for me and rejoice in what it can do for You. Amen.

2

CHOOSING JOY, PEACE, AND HOPE

May the God of hope fill you with all joy and peace
as you trust in him, so that you may overflow
with hope by the power of the Holy Spirit.
ROMANS 15:13 NIV

Father, fill my heart with the absolute joy of Your presence today. Fill me with the peace of Your nature and the unwavering hope for my future. Everywhere I look, it seems I can always find a reason to doubt Your goodness and Your omnipotence. Forgive me for the way I have turned from You in moments of uncertainty. I choose, Lord, to start new and to see these complications as opportunities to trust in You.

I am confident in the joy, peace, and hope You give me through the Holy Spirit. Your unlimited power resides in my heart. Help me access that power to see Your hand in every situation from the wonderful to the heartbreaking. Amen.

3

IN THE WAVES

Immediately Jesus reached out his hand and caught him.
"You of little faith," he said, "why did you doubt?"
MATTHEW 14:31 NIV

Lord, I am like Peter walking to You on the waves. You tell me to take courage and to not be afraid. You tell me to come to You, and I step out of my boat of comfort, of stability. I am so confident and sure of Your power until I focus on the darkness around me, the heartache, and my own sin. Before I know it, I falter. I sink faster every moment I don't trust Your ways.

Forgive me for taking my eyes off You. Forgive me for trying to do things on my own instead of letting You lead. I thank You for always catching me when I fall, for pulling me from the water and the waves of life. Today, Lord, I ask You to help me rely on the truth that I can stand firm in my faith during storms because You are for me.

4

LOVING OTHERS

We love because he first loved us.
1 JOHN 4:19 ESV

Father, sometimes it's hard for me to love the difficult people in my life. They feel like a daily chore I add to my to-do list and check off, and not like a growing relationship. Sometimes we don't agree on the same issue, or they make drastically different decisions than my own. I feel like they never listen to me or respect my feelings. Lord, there are days when I don't believe they deserve my love and forgiveness.

Help me to understand that my ability to love grows from Your love that I am firmly planted in. It shouldn't be about me or what I'm feeling. I know that You forgave my sins on the cross and loved me in my difficult moments. Since this is true, I am confident that I have the ability to love others when it's hard, because it's a reflection of the love You already poured onto me.

5

WHEN I DON'T WANT TO WORK

Work willingly at whatever you do, as though you were working for the Lord rather than for people.
COLOSSIANS 3:23 NLT

*L*ord, there are days when I find myself unmotivated and unwilling to do the work set before me. I am distracted by social media, burdened by circumstances, or uninterested in my current task. How can I find purpose in my jobs for today? How can I convince myself they matter?

Let me remember that I am ultimately working for You. When I focus on You and what You have asked me to do, I can be confident that my work matters. When I don't, I find myself avoiding my responsibilities and making moral compromises.

God, give me an overwhelming sense of duty and pride to know that I am performing for You. Help me return to work with renewed energy, focus, and purpose. The tasks I do and the way I work expand Your kingdom. Amen.

6

WHEN I DON'T UNDERSTAND

I heard, but I did not understand. So I asked,
"My lord, what will the outcome of all this be?"
DANIEL 12:8 NIV

*L*ord, I don't always understand Your ways. Like so many of Your children before me, I want to cry out to ask why. Why is this happening? Why must this hurt? Will it all be worth it?

But I know You mourn with me. I know that You feel every tear I shed and the heartbreaks I go through. I know I can seek Your presence for comfort and rest.

Help me to have faith to trust that You have my life and circumstances in Your hands even when I don't understand. Let me accept that for most of my days, I will never understand why things happen, and allow me to find solace in that. You are in control and working all things for my best interests. Once I am reunited with You, I will see it was all worth it.

7

LOST BUT NOT ALONE

*"For the Son of Man came to seek
and save those who are lost."*
LUKE 19:10 NLT

*L*ord, I remember the day I gave my life to You. I remember the prayer, my testimony of Your greatness. When I was lost in sin, You found me. But there are some days when I still feel hidden in darkness, scrambling for a way out. I make the wrong choice or take the path You didn't want for me. Then I try to redeem myself instead of bringing my sin to You. Forgive me for the embarrassment and shame I let come between us.

Father, You sent Your Son to die for me. I can be assured that His sacrifice covers my sins. I don't need to do anything other than come humbly to Your presence. When I feel I am lost, I know that I don't need to travel far to return to Your loving arms.

8

CONFIDENCE NEEDS CORRECTION

So correct us, GOD, as you see best. Don't lose your temper. That would be the end of us.
JEREMIAH 10:24 MSG

Lord, I know I'm a sinner. I know there are things I struggle with every day that try to set me apart from You and take me away from being like Jesus. These include gossip, lies, pride, selfishness, faithlessness, and other things. To be confident in my relationship with my Creator, I know that I have to be corrected in my daily life. It can be so easy to see someone else's faults before my own.

God, I ask for You to humble me not with anger but with Your everlasting love. I ask for You to open my eyes to what I need to change in my life to be closer to You. I know that correction from a caring Father is good for my physical and spiritual well-being, for when I am corrected and changed by You, I can then be confident in myself.

9

BEING FAITHFUL

By faith Sarah herself received power to conceive,
even when she was past the age, since she
considered him faithful who had promised.
HEBREWS 11:11 ESV

*L*ord, You not only promised Abraham and Sarah a child in their old age, You promised them descendants who would match the number of stars. It took faith for them to believe a blessing like that would come, and they waited a long, long time for it to happen. They made mistakes while waiting, but You still held true to Your word. By their faith, You answered their prayers.

I see myself in them. I want my dreams so strongly, God, and I know the blessings You have promised me. Help me to stay confident in the waiting. I want desperately to act, but You know ultimately what is best for me. I will be faithful to Your timeline because You have been faithful to my needs in the past. When the blessing arrives, I will know I am ready for it.

10

WHEN GOD SAYS NO

For the moment all discipline seems painful rather than pleasant, but later it yields the peaceful fruit of righteousness to those who have been trained by it.
HEBREWS 12:11 ESV

Lord, I don't always understand when You tell me no. I prayed for an outcome many times, and now you ask me to let it go. You ask me to move forward without glancing back. I have to step into complete faith from a place of heartache.

This time is hard for me. I know You will allow me to grieve for what I lost. But I will trust Your ways. You created the heavens and still take time to embrace me in Your love. You are infinite and all-knowing. I choose to be confident that You know what is best for me. While this is painful, You have something greater coming my way.

11

BORN AGAIN

Therefore, if anyone is in Christ, he is a new creation.
The old has passed away; behold, the new has come.
2 Corinthians 5:17 esv

※

Father, there are times when the voice of the enemy reminds me of who I was before Your grace, and it says I'm still that person. It can be so easy to listen to that voice as I battle sin every day and sometimes lose. I find myself wallowing in my shame instead of focusing on Your calling for me.

I need to remember that before anything else, I am Your daughter. My identity is firmly based on Jesus' sacrifice for me and my relationship to Him. I don't have to worry about who I was before, because when You entered my heart, I was born again.

Thank You for making me new. Thank You for washing away my sins so I may live an abundant and healthy life without the pain of my past. I am Yours.

12

WHEN I DON'T FEEL USEFUL

*So they pulled their boats up on shore,
left everything and followed him.*
LUKE 5:11 NIV

*L*ike Simon being called to follow You, I feel inadequate to step forward into the plans You have for me. I'm afraid I'll not be useful because of my age, my talents, the way I look, or my education. Lord, there are so many things that can keep me from following You with my whole heart. Let me stay focused on You and ignore the voices speaking out against me and Your plan. They only block and break me while You give life and direction.

I must remember that my usefulness is linked to my obedience to You. You don't call the prepared, You prepare the called. I can be confident that You have readied me for the tasks You ask of me. This ability to serve and do comes from You and not from me. Thank You, Father, that I can rely on Your everlasting strength.

13

WORTHINESS

To this end we always pray for you, that our God may make you worthy of his calling and may fulfill every resolve for good and every work of faith by his power.

2 THESSALONIANS 1:11 ESV

God, I can get so caught up in the idea that I am not worthy of You, that I am not enough to gain Your promises. But I have to realize that You didn't die for me because of what I can offer to the kingdom. You took on my sin because You loved the world and loved me with an unashamed, full, agape love. That kind of love cannot be measured.

When I ask myself if I am worthy of You, I am trying to measure Your goodness. That is impossible! I feel unworthy because of sin, but Jesus wiped away my sin on the cross and replaced it with immeasurable love. Thank You, Lord, that You remind me daily that when I feel unworthy, You say I'm valuable.

14

SHAME AND FORGIVENESS

*And hope does not put us to shame, because God's
love has been poured out into our hearts through
the Holy Spirit, who has been given to us.*
ROMANS 5:5 NIV

Thank You, God, that You don't put Your children to
shame. You embrace me in my mistakes and forgive
me with boundless love. When Adam and Eve sinned
in Eden, the first thing they felt was shame. That feeling
came from them and the sin they committed, not from
You. You have already paid the price for me. There is
nothing I need to do but to trust You for my repentance.

I believe that I've been forgiven and that You have
remained in me as the Holy Spirit. My shame can
be replaced with the truth that I'm loved and with the
hope that I'm not defined by what I've done in my past.
I am not who I was; I am a child of Yours, redeemed and
cherished.

15

LORD, I'M TIRED

*"Come to me, all you who are weary
and burdened, and I will give you rest."*
MATTHEW 11:28 NIV

Lord, sometimes I feel like I don't have time to even breathe! My days are filled from the moment I wake up until the minute I go to bed. I tell myself I don't have time to rest because there is always one more thing to do, but You did not create Your children to live like this. On the seventh day of Creation, You rested. I can be positive that when I relax, I am not failing. I am preparing for the next task.

Teach me, God, to come to You when I'm tired and when I am overwhelmed. Only when I take the time to be in the presence of the Holy Spirit will I find myself truly refreshed, ready to take on what life has for me next. Help me to remember that You bring the greatest healing renewal.

16

WHEN I WORRY

Give all your worries and cares to God,
for he cares about you.
1 PETER 5:7 NLT

Father, sometimes I don't come to You with all my problems. I'm afraid that my everyday struggles may be insignificant compared to other things happening in the world. I try to deal with them on my own or seek out other comforts. These sometimes don't solve the issue, or they can solve the problem but leave me feeling exhausted.

Thank You, Lord, for reminding me that You care about the details of our lives. You ask us to come to You with every burden, big or small. When we cast our anxieties on You, we can find answers to our problems and peace for our hearts. Today I give all my worries to You. I choose to believe You care deeply and will do what is best for me and the ones I love. I will not focus anymore on the things I ask You to control.

17

FEELING STUPID

Commit yourself to instruction;
listen carefully to words of knowledge.
PROVERBS 23:12 NLT

❧

Father, I feel stupid. Today I don't feel like I'm good enough. When I mess up or make the wrong choice, I'm embarrassed, hurt, and alone. It's hard to remember that other women feel the same way. So many different voices are telling me I need to be the best at every aspect of my life and there's no room for mistakes.

Lord, I am done with trying to be perfect. The pressure that I put on myself is overwhelming and harsh. I know that You don't ask that of me. You ask Your daughters to come broken because only You make things whole. You give us access to ultimate knowledge that the world can't give us or even understand.

If I follow Your Word and commit myself to Your ways, I know that I may make mistakes; but with each prayer, I am becoming the woman You created me to be.

18

MEEK IS NOT WEAK

*But the meek shall inherit the land and
delight themselves in abundant peace.*
PSALM 37:11 ESV

*L*ord, people look at being meek as a weakness, but I know through Jesus it is a sign of power. It is being humble when I could be prideful; it's choosing what God wants before any of my own selfish desires to be seen as strong, independent, and impressive. I can mix up being meek for being weak and think that God isn't allowing me to reach my full potential.

Jesus was confident in Himself because He had full faith in His Father. He was seen as meek because He restrained from using His power for His own good. God, help me be meek for You. I want to be like Jesus and have full confidence in my heavenly Father and not myself. For when I rest in You and stay away from what the world says I should want, I can find everything I need.

19

JEALOUSY

For where you have envy and selfish ambition,
there you find disorder and every evil practice.
JAMES 3:16 NIV

Father, I find myself so jealous of the amazing women You have put in my life. I know it's wrong, but I can't help wanting what they have or to look the way they do. With social media showing their highlights, I think I have to force a happy face to show I'm doing great too. If I let these feelings grow, I might start compromising my morals and ending friendships that could be life-giving.

God, I believe You are what I need. When I start to feel envious of others, let me know that You've given me what I need to do what You've asked me to do. If I'm too busy worrying about others, I will lose sight of my personal walk with You. Without the jealousy, I can be fully confident in You.

20

BEING MEAN

*Be kind to one another, tenderhearted, forgiving
one another, as God in Christ forgave you.*
EPHESIANS 4:32 ESV

In times of stress, I find myself snapping at the people around me. I can be mean and say hurtful things to my friends, family, and coworkers. This comes from my desire to be right, my own pride, and my fear of being intimidated. Father, every day I have to be reminded to love the way Jesus does—with nothing asked in return, to care even when it's hard.

In the end, Jesus did the same for me. Instead of accusing me and leaving me in my sin, He chose to bear it all. He sacrificed Himself not only for me but for all His children. I have no right to treat people any less than that. Help me to be kind and to forgive others when I feel wronged. Instead of lashing out, teach me to speak out of the love You have shown me.

21

WORRIED ABOUT MONEY

The Sovereign LORD is my strength! He makes me as surefooted as a deer, able to tread upon the heights.
HABAKKUK 3:19 NLT

God, Habakkuk lived in a time of uncertainty. He saw his country performing evil deeds and saw how poor they were all becoming. He spoke of barren fields and withering trees. I can't help but relate my life to that picture. Yet Habakkuk still trusted You; he still praised Your name.

Lord, I am so anxious about my financial situation. I feel like I'm working hard and trying my best each day, and I still come up short. Above all, You are my strength and provider. If I rely too heavily on money and my possessions, I will lose confidence in what You have in store for me. Allow me to be aware of my situation but fully focused on You so I will be able to see new doors opening and the eternal life You are creating for me.

22

GOING TO GOD FOR GUILT

*Godly sorrow brings repentance that
leads to salvation and leaves no regret,
but worldly sorrow brings death.*
2 Corinthians 7:10 niv

When I feel guilty, my first instinct is to hide from You, Lord. I forget that You know everything about me and love me anyway. You ask me to come to You for repentance and love while the enemy wants me to stay in darkness.

The fear to approach You in my times of guilt is from my own desire to be perfect. If I rely on this way of thinking, it could lead to even more heartache.

God, it is hard for me to accept that coming to You in my need and hurt isn't a sign of weakness. My strength comes only from You and not from me. While I try to fix my feelings on my own, You offer acceptance and forgiveness. I will rest in that truth today. I am forgiven!

23

SELF-CONTROL

A person without self-control is like
a city with broken-down walls.
PROVERBS 25:28 NLT

Self-control can relate to almost every detail of my life from food to purchases to my feelings and relationships. God, while You created so many amazing things on this earth that are good for us, I know that too much of one thing can be harmful to my body or my use of time.

I know, Father, I'm supposed to choose You above anything else. Self-control is a way I practice wanting You more than the last word, more than one bite, more than another minute. You created me with utmost importance. Self-control helps me to stay faithful to the body and the dreams You have given me.

This control comes from You. I will try my best to reach that power by freely giving up my own and allowing my strength to come from You.

24

GIVING UP CONTROL

*"Therefore do not worry about tomorrow,
for tomorrow will worry about itself.
Each day has enough trouble of its own."*
MATTHEW 6:34 NIV

God, I sometimes wish I could control each day down to the tiniest detail. I want to write down what will happen tomorrow, next week, and even next year. Knowing that some of the plans that I've worked so hard for will change, or not happen, stresses me out. This attitude is affecting me physically and spiritually.

I know, Lord, You ask me not to worry about what will happen in the future. When I take everything into my own hands, I am disobeying You because I'm saying I don't trust You to watch out for me.

I do believe You. Giving up control of my circumstances is what I need to do to show You I am confident in Your ways. I don't need to know what happens next when I'm fully present in a moment that You created for me.

25

WHEN I NEED STRENGTH

*"Don't be dejected and sad, for the joy
of the Lord is your strength!"*
Nehemiah 8:10 nlt

Father, I come to You today and ask for strength. I'm done relying on myself and placing my problems on others. I choose to step out of sadness and hurt into the joy only You give. From this joy comes the strength to finish my day and to get out of bed tomorrow. I can't find that anywhere else but Your presence.

Your daughters don't have to carry the stress of life alone. You give me the gift of the Holy Spirit. You ask me to come to You with all my burdens and doubts and promise to take these on Yourself. Thank You for that today. When I share my load with You, I can be more willing and open to do other tasks set before me.

26

TRUE BEAUTY

*For we are God's handiwork, created in
Christ Jesus to do good works, which
God prepared in advance for us to do.*
EPHESIANS 2:10 NIV

*L*ord, thank You for not looking at outward appearances. While You ask Your daughters to take care of their bodies, You still care about our hearts more. In a world where what I look like is sometimes too important, I know I can rest in Your arms just as I am.

I only need to look at nature to see the beauty You create.

True beauty comes from You. All the products and promises from beauty companies will not bring me any closer to the woman You created me to be. Only a relationship with You can do that. I can be confident in myself when I believe You made every detail of me with a holy purpose in mind.

I may not understand everything You do, but You love me unconditionally. Help me to love myself in that exact same way.

27

THE FRUIT

*But the fruit of the Spirit is love, joy, peace,
patience, kindness, goodness, faithfulness, gentleness,
self-control; against such things there is no law.*
GALATIANS 5:22–23 ESV

*L*ord, I'm not the perfect person I present to the world. There are certain times when I feel like I have to wear a disguise to get through my day. Only You, God, know the real me and accept me as I am. How can I throw away my false face and wear the crown that You give Your children? How can I show people not only the real me but the real You?

Thank You for giving us a list in Your Word of what we gain when we fully trust You. Instead of presenting who I think the world wants, let me show them a daughter who loves and is loved by You. I can do this by practicing the fruit of the Spirit, by diving into time with You. Thank You!

28

CONFIDENCE IN PRAYER

Let us draw near with a true heart in full assurance of faith, with our hearts sprinkled clean from an evil conscience and our bodies washed with pure water.
HEBREWS 10:22 ESV

Father, thank You for Jesus. I know that because of faith in Him, I have access to the presence of God every second of the day. I am never alone. I know with complete trust that You'll answer my prayer. And I know that to pray confidently, I have to come to You with open hands and an open heart, willing to listen to what You have to say. Even if that includes something I don't want to hear.

I know that the key to confident prayer is praising Your name, confessing my sins, and aligning my will with Yours. When I pray, help me to recognize when I take my eyes off You. My first priority is following You and not my own desires. Thank You for being there.

29

GETTING OLDER

Do not say, "Why were the old days better than these?"
For it is not wise to ask such questions.
Ecclesiastes 7:10 niv

L ord, I find myself reaching for what used to be. I tell myself that it was easier and better in my past and that age has only brought hardship. Why can't I go back to who I was? Where is that girl that trusted You so openly?

I know, Father, that You're the One who turns the seasons. I am where I am because You have found it important for me to be here. My age doesn't matter when I look at the eternity I get to spend with You.

I'm confident that every change to my body and circumstances has been ordained in Your will. I embrace the wisdom I have gained over the years, the scars and marks that led me closer to You. When I look at my life as a testament to You, I can embrace who I am.

30

REJECTION

The stone that the builders rejected
has now become the cornerstone.
Psalm 118:22 nlt

God, help me to remember that when I feel rejected, I'm in very good company. Your Son was sent to this earth and rejected by the ones He died for. It gives me comfort to know that my Creator understands my pain and grieves with me through this hurt.

This rejection is leading me closer to the purpose You have given me. I can choose to wallow in this and let it hinder Your plans, or I can keep moving forward with the grace and dignity that You supply to all Your daughters. You don't call us to stay in anger or hurt but to take everything with an understanding that there is more than what this world can give us. Thank You for this protection.

I will keep my gaze set on You and follow Your will above all.

31

SHARING MY STORY

So do not be ashamed of the testimony about our Lord or of me his prisoner. Rather, join with me in suffering for the gospel, by the power of God.
2 Timothy 1:8 niv

Lord, I want to be proud of my testimony. What others may see as a weakness or something shameful, I know led me to the best thing in my life—my relationship with You. I am saved and forgiven under the blood of Jesus. I may be afraid to speak to others or share my story openly, but I know You call Your daughters to do just that.

My words may help another to Christ, and that's the most important thing in the world. Help me to confidently share the wonderful things You have done in my life, unashamed. My story is a testament to Your goodness. I can love those around me by sharing with them the most important news of all—salvation in You.

32

WHEN I AM WEAK

My flesh and my heart may fail, but God is the
strength of my heart and my portion forever.
PSALM 73:26 NIV

Father, I come to You weak to the world around me. Every day I find myself wanting more, giving up pieces of myself for temporary pleasure. I have been trying so hard to move forward, but today I feel like I can't go another step. The enemy says I'm stuck in my sin and will never get out.

Thank You for reminding me that I don't have to do this life alone. You never intended Your daughters to struggle with everything on their own. You are my strength to get through hardships. I hold on to You today and ask for the ability to forgive myself and the power to press onward. Where I am weak, You are strong.

While You ask me to stand firm, I praise You for allowing me to lean on You.

33

ANGER

Be angry and do not sin; do not
let the sun go down on your anger,
and give no opportunity to the devil.
EPHESIANS 4:26–27 ESV

*L*ord, if I'm not careful, I find myself becoming frustrated at so many things throughout my day. It's sometimes easier to lash out at those around me or even You than to figure out what's actually setting me off. I know that it's okay to feel anger at times of injustice and cruelty. You use anger in us to spur Your children into action.

But it's what I do in my anger where I can fall into sin. I realize, Father, that my actions can either harm or help the situation, and choosing Your love in times of resentment can lead to peace, forgiveness, and growth that I can't explain.

Today, I choose Your grace instead of anger. In every situation I will seek Your voice.

34

FINDING JOY

Sorrowful, yet always rejoicing; poor,
yet making many rich; having nothing,
and yet possessing everything.
2 Corinthians 6:10 niv

I know, God, that to be confident, I must be joyful first. No matter what situation I'm in, I should always praise Your name because in You I have all I need. I thank You for the times when choosing joy is easy, and I ask for strength to fight for joy when it's hard.

I believe, Lord, that You are who You say You are. You will do what You say You will. Choosing joy in all circumstances brings me happiness, contentment, and a power to overcome or a peace in waiting.

35

LOVING MYSELF

"The second is equally important:
'Love your neighbor as yourself.' No
other commandment is greater than these."
MARK 12:31 NLT

*L*ord, I know that You call me to love others. It's something we learn when we're little. But I have a hard time starting with me. If I would treat those around me like I treat myself, I wouldn't be a very nice person.

Help me to believe that I am not stupid, worthless, or ugly. Those words have no place in my vocabulary as someone created by You. I am redeemed, worthy, and beautiful.

Seeing myself through the eyes of Jesus is the first step to looking at others that way. This isn't being selfish or prideful; it's a step toward healthy self-love that we are called to as Your daughters. I can't focus on You or others if I only worry about my own life. Shift my view to Yours today, and help me love myself as You do.

36

KEEPING FAITH

*Let love and faithfulness never
leave you; bind them around your neck,
write them on the tablet of your heart.*
PROVERBS 3:3 NIV

Father, let me remember that the amount of my faith in You isn't a matter of when, but a matter of now. All the faith I need to trust Your plan, to be confident in who You made me to be, and to be secure in my salvation is already inside of me.

I don't have to wait to gain the faith that I read about from the heroes of the Bible or I see in the leaders around me. I have their exact same faith from the exact same God. I'm just as special to You as they are, Lord. And You have also created an amazing purpose for me as well!

I will step into that purpose today, God, with complete faith in You.

37

TEMPTED

*When you are tempted, he will show
you a way out so that you can endure.*
1 CORINTHIANS 10:13 NLT

God, You have truly blessed me with so many wonderful experiences. But sometimes the brokenness of this life can distort these countless good things. Temporary pleasure becomes more important than obedience, and I find myself reaching for things to fill me up instead of You. These opportunities can be so harmful to my well-being.

I am tempted every day to turn my back on You to choose my worldly desires. Giving my life to You was not a promise that challenges were over. But it is a promise that I wouldn't have to go through them alone. Forgive me for the times I fell into temptation and sinned. Thank You for always providing strength and a way out. I don't have to rely on my own willpower. Next time I find myself tempted, I will look to You.

38

THE PLAN

"For I know the plans I have for you,
declares the LORD, plans for welfare and
not for evil, to give you a future and a hope."
JEREMIAH 29:11 ESV

Father, I don't have to go through life wondering if You created me with a purpose. You tell me in Your Word time and time again that You have plans for me that are better than I could ever dream up myself. On the days I am lost and unhappy and I wonder if I'm doing the right thing, I will praise You.

Lord, I choose the hope You give me in every situation and decision. I may be doubtful of my path, but instead of focusing on relief from my troubles or on my dreams coming true, I will remember what You have already done for me, not what You can do for me. What's meant to be will happen in a time perfected by Your hands. Thank You!

39

WHEN I AM OVERWHELMED

*When I am overwhelmed, you alone
know the way I should turn.*
PSALM 142:3 NLT

*L*ord, I'm confident that You are leading me where I need to go. Through trials and hardships, through days of calm, You show me the way. If I keep following Your teachings and spending time with You, I know the choices I make will align with Your will. And if they don't, I believe You will cover me with Your wonderful grace. Sometimes I won't even have the answer, but it will be an opportunity to trust.

You have not forgotten me or my prayers.

Thank You for giving me rest when I am tired and overwhelmed. While You give Your daughters free will, I am so thankful that I don't have to make decisions on my own. I will take time today to access the peace the Holy Spirit has bestowed on me, and I will do my best to do Your will.

40

PERSECUTION

"Though he slay me, I will hope in him;
yet I will argue my ways to his face."
JOB 13:15 ESV

Lord, Your Word says we will be persecuted for believing in You. We may miss out on opportunities, relationships, and more for the sake of Your name. I find myself feeling left out and lonely. Sometimes I'm even scared to say that I am a Christ-follower or share my story with nonbelievers.

Job was persecuted on all sides. Where he was supposed to find comfort, he found pain. His wife told him to curse Your name. But he stood upright and strong in his struggles and praised You.

I will do my best, God, to do the same. When I feel pressed, I will lean on You for comfort. When I feel alone, I will relish in Your presence. I know that being persecuted has nothing to do with me; it's a chance to confidently show the world around me Your grace.

WORKING TOWARD PURPOSE

So I decided there is nothing better than to enjoy food and drink and to find satisfaction in work. Then I realized that these pleasures are from the hand of God.
ECCLESIASTES 2:24 NLT

God, I shouldn't feel guilty about enjoying the earthly things You have blessed me with. These things I love, like my hobbies or my job, come from You. While there are days when I and my work feel meaningless, I know that it is all coming together for Your purpose. When I feel like I'm not where I am supposed to be, please lead me in the right direction.

Help me remember that my work is never meaningless when it is in pursuit of the Lord's glory. I know that my desire to do what You've called me to do comes from the Holy Spirit. Doing it on my own is not enough. Thank You for creating me and the things in my life to enjoy!

42

SALVATION IN JESUS

*"Salvation is found in no one else,
for there is no other name under heaven
given to mankind by which we must be saved."*

Acts 4:12 NIV

Jesus, I know there is no way to save myself except through You. Everything I do means nothing if I haven't fully given myself to You and accepted that You have brought me eternal life by the sacrifice on the cross. I can't buy my salvation or work my way into heaven. Thank You for covering my sins and paying my way.

I have given my heart to Jesus; therefore, I can be confident that I have a place waiting for me after death. I'll try my best to live today like a woman freed from her chains. Because of You, I'm no longer lost in darkness but bathed in warm, loving light. I walk in Your promises today as Your daughter, saved and adored.

43

JUDGING OTHERS

May God, who gives this patience and encouragement,
help you live in complete harmony with each other,
as is fitting for followers of Christ Jesus.
ROMANS 15:5 NLT

*L*ord, I can be so quick to judge those around me before I know the whole story. I find myself thinking that I'm better than others because of who I am and what I have. I think just because I am a Christian, I deserve more things out of this life than some people around me.

You ask me to love others as You have loved Your children, forgiving them as You have forgiven me. We are all the same in Your eyes, Father.

Grant me peace to view situations with the same loving, unbiased eyes. Give me encouragement to actively invest in those You have put in my life. You sent Your Son to die for all of us, not just me. Today I will try my best to treat everyone as the gift they are.

44

GENTLENESS

Let your gentleness be evident
to all. The Lord is near.
PHILIPPIANS 4:5 NIV

I have such a hard time controlling my reactions, Lord. It's so much easier to blow up in anger and hurt someone who has wronged me than to actually get to the bottom of the issue and seek forgiveness on both sides. I hate to admit I'm wrong. I hate to say I'm hurt.

But I know, Father, that You call Your daughters to be gentle in all situations. This type of grace that I show during conflicts is evidence of Your peace. If I follow You, I have a duty to show others Your character. You are not unkind or impatient. You don't keep a record of wrongs.

Be near me during chaos as I try to seek the comfort and answers You provide. My strength and hope are only a prayer away. You promise to be near every second of the day.

45

SURRENDER

*"Whoever finds their life will lose it, and whoever
loses their life for my sake will find it."*
MATTHEW 10:39 NIV

Jesus, what is holding me back from You? Instead of moving steadfast into a future with You, I find myself standing still on the sidelines. Am I scared of the changes following You will bring? Am I unwilling to give up the things I have?

Take a look at my life, and humble me. I'm sorry for the areas that I've kept separate from my journey with You. I give these areas over to You today and ask for direction. Lord, the plans You have for me are greater than I can imagine, and giving all my life over is a step closer to seeing it's better Your way.

It may be hard, and it will hurt, but choosing You above all is worth it. I surrender everything to You. Amen.

46

GOOD ENOUGH

Remember, dear brothers and sisters,
that few of you were wise in the world's eyes
or powerful or wealthy when God called you.
1 Corinthians 1:26 nlt

*L*ord, I don't feel good enough. You call me to do these amazing things, and I don't think I'm the person You need. There are others with more faith, more money, more power than me. Help me to remember that You don't view the world as we do. Worldly possessions and social class don't matter to the plans You have.

I know I'm focusing on what I can do and not what You provide to me. Everything I need to fulfill what You have asked of me is available in the Holy Spirit within me.

God, let me feel that confidence today. Grant me the power to step forward into my calling. When I am fully reliant on You, I don't have to worry about not being good enough.

47

I AM PRECIOUS

"Don't be afraid," he said, "for you are very
precious to God. Peace! Be encouraged! Be strong!"
DANIEL 10:19 NLT

God, thank You for reminding me every day how precious and important I am to You. The Creator of the seas and the mountains, the birds and the winds, wanted someone like me on this earth too. I match the most beautiful creations of nature.

From my relationship with You, I have endless peace, encouragement, and strength. Thank You for those gifts. I can be confident in myself because I know You're proud of Your daughter and ask me to abide in what the Spirit gives.

I won't be afraid of what comes in the future because I know You're sovereign. I will reach into those truths of peace and strength today. Thank You for always being there and for Your endless comfort.

48

GIVING ALL

"Then all the nations will call you blessed, for yours will be a delightful land," says the LORD Almighty.
MALACHI 3:12 NIV

*L*ord, You ask me to give all to You. This includes my time and talents, my dreams and ideas. You don't do this selfishly, though some days I am bound to think so. Forgive me for thinking You take things to punish or hurt me.

You ask for my life because You know things that I do not. You know the blessings I can have if I only give up control. When I'm in pain because I feel You have taken away my dreams, I choose to believe that You still know best.

Trusting You is the only way to get through loss and hardship. When I give all to You and trust You with reckless abandon, I will be able to see the blessings around me and the delights of my life with You. I need nothing else but You.

HEAVEN-FOCUSED

*But do not overlook this one fact, beloved,
that with the Lord one day is as a thousand
years, and a thousand years as one day.*
2 PETER 3:8 ESV

*L*ord, keep me heaven-focused. Help me remember that my days in this world are timed perfectly by You. My embarrassments, moments of weakness, and disappointments are insignificant when I look at what I have waiting for me: an eternity with You.

Those times are hard to put into perspective, but if I look at them with Your eyes, I'll see how they are helping me become the woman You want me to be. Time can feed our need for control, and I can be addicted to how time defines standards in my life. You are more important to me, Lord.

I will start viewing my days as You ask us to—a day to serve You and a day closer to forever in heaven.

50

THE SHAPE I'M IN

*The sun has one kind of glory, while the moon
and stars each have another kind. And even
the stars differ from each other in their glory.*
1 CORINTHIANS 15:41 NLT

Thank You, God, that the body I have every season
is a chance to represent Your glory. The body I had
growing up showed Your attention to detail, evolving
into the person I am today. The body I have now is an
opportunity to show Your grace and mercy. The body I
will have with You in heaven will show Your magnificence in an oh-so-beautiful way.

Whether I'm proud of the shape I'm in or not, I
can be thankful that You are a provider of wonderful
things and an artist beyond my imagination. Help me
to be kind to my body and to the ladies around me. We
are all fighting battles, and sometimes our bodies show
more than we want to the rest of the world. Let us fight
together.

51

MAKING DECISIONS

*"Seek first the kingdom of God and his righteousness,
and all these things will be added to you."*
MATTHEW 6:33 ESV

Father, I have to make a choice. It is so important and will not only affect me but my loved ones as well. The worry of making it has affected every second of my life, and I can't live in it anymore. I'm scared to make the wrong decision, so I reach out to You now for guidance, wisdom, and peace. With study in Your Word and time in Your presence, I know that mere act of simply seeking Your plan will delight You.

When I finally have Your answer, I will not hesitate to follow through. I will be true to my word. Fill me with peace as I give the situation over to You. Once I have made the best decision I could, promise to take it from there. Thank You for making our burdens light.

52

SUBMITTING

Submit to one another out of reverence for Christ.
EPHESIANS 5:21 NIV

*L*ord, help me remember that You created authority. I know I've been letting rebellion slip into my relationship with You. Forgive me.

Sometimes I find myself disregarding rules or regulations because I feel like I'm an exception to it. The brokenness of sin has distorted the truth, and my individual judgment has become more important to me than the fact that You are in control. Submitting to others is not weakness; it's an act of loving others because they are worthy of it by being Your children. It is being like Jesus.

I pray for Your followers to practice mutual submission every day. Help me to set my own interests aside and support the talents and plans of others. If I turn away from what only I want, I can focus on building Your kingdom on earth.

53

PROMISED

*GOD said, "My presence will go with you.
I'll see the journey to the end."*
EXODUS 33:14 MSG

Father, I'm in a season of waiting. Like the Israelites wandering the desert, I feel like I will never see the Promised Land. Sometimes I become so fixated on the final destination, I forget what I can learn on the journey. I'm sorry for becoming obsessed with what You have promised me instead of focusing on my relationship with You.

You are my beginning and end and everything in between. You have promised me wonderful things, but they ultimately mean nothing without Your presence. Thank You for following through when I am foolish, when I sin, or when I pull away from You. I don't deserve Your greatness.

I want to take time to be with You in thankfulness. I realize that You are what You have promised. I am confident that You are all I need.

54

FRIENDSHIP

Two are better off than one, for they
can help each other succeed.
ECCLESIASTES 4:9 NLT

Relationships can be scary. From romances to friend-ships to family ties, when I open my heart to some-one, I always risk getting hurt. Lord, let me remember that I'm not called to a life of aloneness because it's eas-ier. I'm called to love others like Jesus. For support, un-derstanding and love, You want me to surround myself with people who love Christ.

When You're at the forefront of my mind, a rela-tionship doesn't become a hardship, though some may feel like one. I can be confident everyone is in my life for a reason. I'll learn from many and grow with them into the woman You created me to be. Thank You for the re-lationships I have and for the ones I'll gain in the future. I'll keep You at the heart of all of them.

55

SPEAKING FROM THE LORD

The wise in heart accept commands,
but a chattering fool comes to ruin.
PROVERBS 10:8 NIV

*L*ord, help me to know when to speak and when to hold my tongue. It feels so good to have the last word or to add my thoughts to conversations, but I know that seeking Your voice in every communication is the best way to go. Only when my words are truthful and loving are they appropriate.

I can be prideful when someone takes my advice or when I win an argument. I'm sorry for the times I spoke out of my own selfishness or anger.

Give me a heart, God, that longs for Your wisdom. I want to be confident in the things I say by knowing they have come from a place fully invested in the Spirit. When I speak, I want it to be according to the will that is above mine.

56

PRAISE HIS NAME

*Praise be to the LORD, the God of Israel,
from everlasting to everlasting. Then all the
people said "Amen" and "Praise the LORD."*
1 CHRONICLES 16:36 NIV

Lord, thank You for the wonders of this life. Thank You for Your endearing love and all You have created for me. I can't even comprehend Your endlessness because measuring Your love for me is like Abraham counting the stars.

I won't be afraid to share You with the rest of the world. When others ask me about my joy and peace, I will answer confidently that it comes from You. If I only rely on myself, I grow tired or become frustrated, but I always find comfort and renewal in Your presence.

I praise Your name and worship You today in whatever I do. Thank You for allowing me a piece of forever in my life through our relationship.

57

TRUE WEALTH

Whoever loves money never has enough;
whoever loves wealth is never satisfied with
their income. This too is meaningless.
ECCLESIASTES 5:10 NIV

Lord, turn my focus from material things and toward You. While this world measures me by the money I have and the things I own, You measure my heart. Thank You, Father. Thank You for loving me the best above all. I hope my heart reflects Your Son's.

You tell us that we don't get to take anything with us when we die. I hope I leave my worth in what I did for You and with the people I loved instead of in a bank.

You are all I need, God. Money is important to survive, but I want my attention to be on more than survival. You call me to a life of thriving and that can only happen when my heart is full of You and not of things that fade away.

58

WONDER

*Everyone was gripped with great wonder and
awe, and they praised God, exclaiming,
"We have seen amazing things today!"*
LUKE 5:26 NLT

God, Thank You for sending Jesus. Through His name, You have poured out forgiveness on me when I don't deserve it. Jesus is not only a healer and a miracle worker, He is my Savior. Even today, when I feel so distant from what happened in the Bible, Jesus still heals. He still performs miracles. And when I let Him, He saves me from sin, shame, loneliness, heartache, and more.

I have wonder and awe when I think of Jesus. Don't let me lose that childlike faith and astonishment in You, God! When I keep that mindset, I can always be sure that You'll come through for me. Every outcome is a win when I look at the bigger picture of my life.

59

WITHHOLDING GOOD

*Do not withhold good from those to whom
it is due, when it is in your power to do it.*
PROVERBS 3:27 ESV

Father, I sometimes find myself wanting to withhold amazing things from others because I feel like they don't deserve it or I'm jealous I've never gotten the same treatment. This can include praise, attention, help, and so on. I can get stuck in the worldly mindset of looking out for myself first. I shouldn't shy away from helping people because of what they do and how it makes me feel.

God, You call us to be giving no matter what our circumstances may be. I'm sorry for only noticing what I want when there are so many amazing people blessing me each day. Open my eyes to the needs around me, and give me the courage to do whatever I can for others. You have given me grace and power to do such things. Thank You!

60

TRUSTING GOD'S TIMING

Even though he should live a thousand
years twice over, yet enjoy no good—
do not all go to the one place?
ECCLESIASTES 6:6 ESV

God, remind me daily that I have time. Sometimes I'm forced to believe the idea that I need to have so many accomplishments by a certain age. I feel like my life has to look a certain way, and I don't think I'm living up to those certain standards.

If I don't fully focus on You and the good things You have provided, I could live forever and never be satisfied. Your timing is perfect, Father, and You know best. Instead of worrying about what I am to the world, I will start working on where I am in Your heart. I'm confident in Your timing, and I can be sure of the life I'm living and the work I'm doing. I know it's all in Your plan.

61

COME WITH ME

*After this he went out and saw a man named
Levi at his work collecting taxes. Jesus said,
"Come along with me." And he did—walked
away from everything and went with him.*
LUKE 5:27–28 MSG

No one is too far from Your love, God. When I'm
at my darkest, You keep asking me to follow You.
Despite what I have done and the burdens I carry, You
ask me to follow You. But there is a price in choosing
that. I have to leave the old me behind, walk away from
the things I've done on my own, the path I thought I
would take.

This can be so hard, Father, stepping away from
what I have always known. But I trust You will be there
beside me every step of the way. No one is unusable by
the Lord, including me. Help me walk into my destiny
today, following my Savior.

62

REACH AND RECEIVE

*"Whoever receives one such child in my name
receives me, and whoever receives me,
receives not me but him who sent me."*

MARK 9:37 ESV

*L*ord, let me never stop reaching for You like a child reaches for a parent. When I'm stressed, I find calm. When I'm angry, I gain peace. When I'm hurt, I find comfort. I'm confident that each time I call Your name, You will answer and I will receive.

When I see myself as Your child, I feel free to come to You with everything: my hurts and my good news. Like any toddler, I want to share. Thank You for allowing me to be in constant companionship with You. You listen to even the smallest prayer.

Open my eyes to who may need this news today. Each one of Your children deserves a chance to give their life to You and gain this abundant life I have. I would be humbled to be a part of it.

63

PRAISE

There the Israelites sang this song:
"Spring up, O well! Yes, sing its praises!"
NUMBERS 21:17 NLT

*L*ord, how You love to hear me praise You, and how much I love to worship You. Not for the things You have done in my life but for being my God. You guide, You conquer, and You provide. You answer, You discipline, and You protect. Thank You!

Forgive me for not taking time to sit in the wonders of You and proclaim Your goodness to the world. Today, I choose to praise in every season and situation because the greatest thing You could do for me has already been done: Jesus saved me and took my sin away so I can spend eternity in heaven.

That alone deserves all my devotion. When the well is running, I will worship. When the well is dry, I will praise. I am not confident in the well. I trust the One who brings the water.

64

GOD STANDS FOREVER

*"The grass withers and the flowers fade,
but the word of our God stands forever."*
ISAIAH 40:8 NLT

*L*ord, help me to remember that You are everlasting. While nature shifts with the seasons, relationships ebb, and looks fade with the years, You are forever unchanging. Although the words and beliefs of people can be altered from day to day, Your Word stands firm and is always true. It never falters or lies.

I can't rely on the things of this world, but I can continually turn to You and scripture for all I need. What brings me temporary comfort today is no match for the love You provide to me.

Let me be sure of that today. Give me the peace and knowledge that while this world is temporary, You have created eternity for me. Thank You.

65

COMFORTING FRIENDS

Rejoice with those who rejoice;
mourn with those who mourn.
ROMANS 12:15 NIV

*L*ord, guide me in saying the right things to my friends no matter what season they're in. When they are happy, let me share in that happiness with no ounce of envy. When they are sad, help me to bring them comfort.

I can't always control what happens to me or those I love, but I can control how I respond to them. When jealousy spikes, I will remember what You have already given me. When I feel like I can't speak to their grief, allow my presence to be enough.

God, You do the same for me every day. In my highs and lows, You are there. Because You first comforted and loved me, I have the chance to love others with the same big, agape love. I am not asking to be their only support; I pray my example points them toward You.

66

FLOURISHING

*The godly will flourish like palm trees
and grow strong like the cedars of Lebanon.*
PSALM 92:12 NLT

Father, I know that You want to see me prosper, sharing goodness and grace with those who see me. However, there are so many things in this life that can keep me from becoming the woman You want me to be. I make idols out of people and possessions. Feelings and thoughts get distorted in selfishness. I rely on myself more than the power I can gain from the Holy Spirit. I'm sorry.

I trust, Lord, that if I stick to Your ways, I will grow to be more like Jesus every day. If I follow the ways of this world, they will lead me further from You. Help me to notice when I'm more focused on this life than on my place in heaven. When I glean my purpose from You, I truly flourish into the best version of me.

67

DOWNWARD

*"I did find this: God created people to
be virtuous, but they have each turned
to follow their own downward path."*
ECCLESIASTES 7:29 NLT

God, I know that You created me to be like You. I was meant to be good and honest with no leaning toward wrong. But I live in a broken world and battle sin that pulls me away from You. Sin is so enticing, Father, and promises me things that aren't true. I'm sorry I fall for it in hopes I can get what I want and somehow get away with it.

You know my heart and love me anyway. You choose to forgive me when I have a hard time forgiving myself. Thank You for the chance I have to be virtuous through You. When I count on my own virtue, I will fail; but when my self-control comes from You, I am supernaturally powerful. Thank You, Lord, that I don't have to fight sin alone.

68

SEXUAL IMAGES

*"I say to you that everyone who looks at
a woman with lustful intent has already
committed adultery with her in his heart."*
MATTHEW 5:28 ESV

God, I know that women fight the same sexual
struggles that men do. Every day I am hounded by
images of sex in the media, and I am tempted to fall
for its temporary pleasure. You created sex to be wonderful and enjoyable for us, but You have also made boundaries around it, so I can enjoy it in the most healthy and
best ways with someone You created for me. When we
spend time on these images from the world, the version
of sex and intimacy You created, Lord, can be distorted.

I long for the intimacy and relationship sex can
bring, but I want it in the way You designed. Give me
the strength to overcome my desire and the wisdom and
character to protect my heart.

69

COURAGE FOR FAITH

Peter and the other apostles replied:
"We must obey God rather than human beings!"
ACTS 5:29 NIV

*L*ord, I want the confidence to stand up for Jesus. The apostles were sure that their Savior had triumphed over His oppressors and death. They were unmoving in their mission to serve their God and their Friend. Let me access that faith today! When I worry about sharing Your story, it's because I'm scared of what this world will say about me. But my value is not of this life; it is found in Christ.

Grant me the courage to follow You and speak Your love. Empower me with the Holy Spirit to do the work set before me. I don't want to back down from what I believe in, but give me wisdom to know the difference between Your truth and mine. Help me to access unlimited faith to stand for You and never renounce Your glorious name.

70

NOT OF FEAR

*For God gave us a spirit not of fear
but of power and love and self-control.*
2 Timothy 1:7 esv

This is what I know You give me, Father: unlimited power, abounding love, unmoving self-control. Nowhere in Your Word do You say You grant me fear. Why then do I feel it constantly? Why is fear such a natural state for me that I have forgotten what it's like to live free in You?

I want to live fearlessly, Lord. I want to be forever courageous and faithful. When I live that way, I can confidently master the plans You have for me. Heartache doesn't last as long because I know You have so much more created for me. If I am ruled by fear, I may never find my destiny.

I ask for courage today from the source of all good things. I am unstoppable with You.

71

PROVIDING

*He said to his disciples, "Therefore I tell you,
do not be anxious about your life, what you will
eat, nor about your body, what you will put on."*
LUKE 12:22 ESV

God, how can You tell us not to worry? There are people who do not have enough to eat, clothes to wear, or a home to return to. How can You say to those who are hurting in this way not to be anxious?

I know, Lord, that once again You're asking me to turn my gaze toward You. Jesus is telling me not to rely on myself to gain these things. It is about trusting God to provide for His children. You don't promise me unlimited riches, but You promise to care for me day to day.

So, take care of me, Father. Look out for my loved ones and those who need Your help. Thank You for loving me thoroughly and providing for me when I need Your help.

72

ACTS OF CHARITY

"Be careful not to practice your righteousness in front of others to be seen by them. If you do, you will have no reward from your Father in heaven."
MATTHEW 6:1 NIV

Father, it feels good when I'm acknowledged for the things I do. I'm sorry my pride gets the better of me and I do deeds for others only so I can feel good about myself. You call me to love others so I can point them back to You. I know that it isn't about me at all.

Use me each day to be a blessing to someone in need. Give me the eyes to see where I'm needed. Allow me to humbly love others with the pure intention of doing Your good work in the world and leading those hurting to the story of the cross.

I can help others because I was first helped by You, loved endlessly by You. Thank You!

73

COMPASSION

*Finally, all of you, be like-minded, be sympathetic,
love one another, be compassionate and humble.*
1 PETER 3:8 NIV

*L*ord, I want to have compassion like Jesus, to love selflessly as I've been loved by You. When I asked You into my heart, I was filled with the Holy Spirit, a source of all the good things that You give me. If I try to love fully on my own, I'm lacking. But when I love from the Holy Spirit in me, my reach can be endless.

Loving out of true compassion isn't about drawing attention to myself or staying on the sidelines or behind social media posts. It is about actively praying to You and then going out to fill a need. Where are You needed, Lord? What can I do to serve Your children?

God, keep me humble. Let me be empathetic to the heartache I see around me. Give me the courage to serve others. Amen.

74

REVENGE

Don't let evil conquer you,
but conquer evil by doing good.
ROMANS 12:21 NLT

L ord, I get so angry when I see injustice in this world. How do I fight oppression in Your name? You never ask me to be a judge or an avenger. You call me to love. You tell me to serve my enemies when I can, not out of anger or aggression but out of selfless, blood-bought love.

This can be so hard, Lord. And to be honest, I don't want to help others I know have done harm. But I'm confident that You will make everything right. I am called to share the Gospel as best I can and follow the voice of Jesus in every situation I face.

Grant me the goodness of Your heart, Lord. Keep my frustration in check so that when I get to heaven, You will be able to say I was a daughter after her Father's heart and honorable to those around her.

75

UNCHANGING

Every good gift and every perfect gift is from above, coming down from the Father of lights, with whom there is no variation or shadow due to change.
JAMES 1:17 ESV

Lord, so many things in my life are changing. I'm getting older every day. My relationships are shifting. Nothing in my life is constant even though I wish it could be. But I thank You today that You're unchanging. The Lord in the Bible is still the Lord right now. The Jesus I gave my life to and worship is the Jesus that rose again. Your plans, character, and promises will always be the same.

In this way, I know that I can trust You. When life gets out of hand and I feel like I'm losing control, I know that You have full authority. While change may affect others, I won't be shaken. Thank You for that gift.

76

CARRYING BURDENS

Carry each other's burdens, and in this
way you will fulfill the law of Christ.
GALATIANS 6:2 NIV

Give me a passion for helping people, God. I commit my life to be more like Jesus. When I don't want to help others, when it's hard for me, ignite me with a fire to spread Your love. There is so much prejudice and injustice in this world, and it can sometimes be scary. I even ask myself if I can really make a difference.

But You don't ask me to stay silent because of fear. You don't ask me to make a difference for my own sake. You call me to love others and to help carry burdens.

Help me to recognize those around me who need help carrying the hardships of life. I don't want to turn blindly from those in need. As Jesus has helped lighten my load, let me confidently be a servant to others.

WHEN I WAS IN DARKNESS

He brought me out into a broad place;
he rescued me, because he delighted in me.
PSALM 18:19 ESV

*L*ord, thank You for rescuing me when I didn't even know I needed saving. I spent so much time in the darkness, I forgot light exists. I forgot there were other ways to live. I became used to the pain, the heartache. I wore it like a badge of honor, an excuse to sin, for reasons to stay in my comfortable misery.

I breathe in Your presence like fresh air, reminded of peace, joy, comfort, and love. Wrap me in Your arms so I can feel safe once again. I have spent too much time in the dark, and I want to bask in Your light, Father. I long to feel Your unlimited goodness.

I'm sorry for my time away from You. I know I am forgiven and washed in the blood. Remind me daily that I don't have to live in darkness ever again.

WHEN I AM IN DARKNESS

But me he caught—reached all the way from sky to sea;
he pulled me out of that ocean of hate, that enemy
chaos, the void in which I was drowning.
PSALM 18:16–17 MSG

I am in a dark season of life, Lord. I look around, and I can't see a future or a reason for all of this. I can't see Your goodness. But I can feel fear. I am scared, angry, lost, and heartbroken. Why aren't You here, God? Why can't I see Your hands working or Your heart beating?

Pull me out of this darkness. Hold me close to light and love. This hurt feels like waves breaking over me again and again. Every time I reach comfort, I am plunged back into despair. Control this storm, Father. Call out its name and show Your power.

You are my Savior and my stronghold. I am confident You will save me, Lord, according to Your will. Be with me now, Jesus.

79

ASSURANCE

When Christ, who is your life, appears,
then you also will appear with him in glory.
COLOSSIANS 3:4 NIV

Thank You, God, for sending Jesus to die for me. Thank You for the amazing moment of resurrection and for conquering death. With the victory comes grace for me even though I don't deserve it. I get to share that miracle with You every day of my life. Thank You, Father!

The enemy tries to cheat this and tell me that I'm not saved. "How could someone like you possibly be saved by Him?" he says. But it is never about me, Lord. It's about Your boundless love for me. You will not leave me behind.

I will believe Your truth instead of choosing the enemy's lies. I will be confident in the fact I have a heavenly home waiting for me and that death is not an end but a new beginning.

80

LOVE MY BODY

Therefore, I urge you, brothers and sisters, in view of God's mercy, to offer your bodies as a living sacrifice, holy and pleasing to God—this is your true and proper worship.
ROMANS 12:1 NIV

*L*ord, my body is amazingly designed. Not only was it made for me to live an abundant life, it was created as a sacrifice to You, a way to worship. My body is not my own but ultimately Yours to use.

You created my body and asked me to take care of it. Physically, I have the chance to show the world Your glory. So, give me the strength to stay away from temptations and actions that could cause harm to Your creation.

God, I pray to be willing to accept the things I can't change about myself. And I hope You will give me the self-control, endurance, and willpower to correct things I can. I want to start living fully in the way You created me.

MENTORING

Fathers, do not aggravate your children,
or they will become discouraged.
COLOSSIANS 3:21 NLT

God, allow me to always be encouraging to the young people in my life. If You have asked me to be a spiritual mentor to them, I want to be the best I can be. There will always be disappointments and hardships in this world, and I don't want to ever be a reason someone hurts. You boost my confidence, Lord, and I want to inspire the women around me to be happy with the way You made them too.

Remind me to think before I speak or act, constantly seeking Your way, letting Your love and truth flow through my words and actions. Allow me to be empathetic to their problems and circumstances, willing to counsel when wanted and willing to listen when needed.

I pray that, instead of relying on me, they grow ever closer to You. Please let them seek Your wisdom and find comfort in Your arms. Amen.

82

SLIPPING

When I said, "My foot is slipping,"
your unfailing love, LORD, supported me.
PSALM 94:18 NIV

*L*ord, when I feel like I can't finish the task set before me, I know Your strength will help me persevere. When I am falling into temptation or losing my grip on difficult emotions, I know that You'll provide stability and a foundation to stand on.

You have given me godly relationships for accountability and the overwhelming presence of Your Holy Spirit in every moment of life. I never have to deal with difficulties on my own. Thank You for that. I'm confident that when I admit I am weak, You will be strong.

God, open my eyes to the times I am prideful and try to save myself. Forgive me for the times I have done so in the past. Humble me so I can fulfill Your plans for me with grace and love.

83

BELIEVE IN HIS PROMISES

*"Everyone who lives in me and believes in me will
never ever die. Do you believe this, Martha?"*
JOHN 11:26 NLT

God, thank You for sending Your Son. He experienced everything I'll go through in my life. In this truth, I know I can trust Him when I read that He mourns and rejoices with us. You do amazing things for me, and all You ask of me in return is to have faith.

Sometimes it is hard to understand Your promises when I live in a world so full of broken ones. You tell me I am loved and bought with a price. If I have given my heart over to Jesus, I won't spiritually die but have eternity in heaven. I will see my Savior. I want faith, Lord, to be confident that is true.

When I worry if I'll get to see You in heaven, grant me peace to know that what You say is always true.

84

NO EXPECTATIONS

*Therefore encourage one another and build
one another up, just as you are doing.*
1 THESSALONIANS 5:11 ESV

God, aid me in building up those around me. I feel like I'm not getting the same encouragement in return, so let me remember where my worth is really found—in You. Loving while expecting something in return is not the unbreakable, agape love You ask me to give. You cover me in unmeasurable adoration and forgiveness, no matter what I have done. I want to love others that way.

When I'm confident in the way I am and what I do, pulling from Your Spirit inside me, I can love and encourage others in the same way without wanting anything in return. Allow Your grace and presence to be enough for me.

It can be tiring to always be positive without being encouraged in return. I will seek comfort and rest in You today. Thank You for always being there when I need to be built up.

85

WHOLEHEARTEDLY

*In everything that he undertook in the service
of God's temple and in obedience to the law and
the commands, he sought his God and worked
wholeheartedly. And so he prospered.*

2 CHRONICLES 31:21 NIV

Lord, I want to be confident in the daily work You have called me to. I know that if I seek Your will, follow Your commandments, and work with a full heart, I will prosper. This doesn't mean my life will be absent of trouble or that I will get everything I want, but I'll be living the best possible life You want for me.

Help me, God, to do everything You want me to do wholeheartedly. This means the menial tasks at my job, loving those who make it hard to, and moving forward when I don't feel like it. I know I'm working for You, and when others see me walking with a full heart, I want to be able to tell them why.

ARGUMENTS

Again I say, don't get involved in foolish,
ignorant arguments that only start fights.
2 TIMOTHY 2:23 NLT

*L*ord, give me wisdom when to defend myself and when to step away from petty arguing. Don't let me fall into the traps the enemy sets that can cause me to become frustrated and angry with others. Little issues have ruined too many good relationships.

You don't ask me to fight over insignificant issues but to love those around me as well as I can. The only real arguments I should have are to be centered on issues near to Your heart, and our side must always point to Your grace and truth. We must approach the other side humbly, with the words and ways of Jesus and how He battled diversity.

Thank You, Father, for giving me a powerful voice to use. Direct my words in loving ways. Grant me the confidence to always use it well.

87

TOSSED BY WIND

But when you ask, you must believe and not doubt,
because the one who doubts is like a wave of
the sea, blown and tossed by the wind.
JAMES 1:6 NIV

*L*ord, let me have a strong faith, willing to accept whatever You allow to come my way. Take away all my doubts and uncertainties when it comes to Your plan for me. When I pray about decisions, I know You hear me and will answer. All You ask of me in return is my unwavering belief. I want to turn away from the false idols of today for wisdom.

If I go to other sources for my answers, I will always be changing my mind or unsure of what to do next. If I'm not fully grounded in You, life will always find ways to toss me around like the wind tosses waves.

I choose to trust in You with all my being. With my belief in You, I cannot be moved.

88

A SHIELD

But you, O LORD, are a shield about me,
my glory, and the lifter of my head.
PSALM 3:3 ESV

Thank You, God, for calling out to me through my sin. Thank You for surrounding me with unyielding love and protection when I returned the call. Something is happening in my life that brings uncertainty and fear. I don't know what's going to happen. You know, Father, what it is and whom it will affect.

I ask You now, Lord, for a shield of protection around me. I ask for Your guiding hand to come down, Father. I have limits; I'm weak, but You are strong. Your miracles are limitless.

Give me confidence to trust Your ways. Give me faith to believe in Your protection. Your shield is unbreakable against my enemies. Thank You for being with me and bringing me comfort. I praise Your name as I wait for You.

89

SPEECHLESS

"But now, since you didn't believe what I said, you will be silent and unable to speak until the child is born. For my words will certainly be fulfilled at the proper time."
LUKE 1:20 NLT

*L*ord, I don't want to ever speak harshly against Your name. My human nature can be so prone to doubt. Like Zechariah being told about his child, my worldly standards sometimes can't comprehend Your miracles. When You promise something into my life, my first instinct is to doubt because of other disappointments.

But You are always truthful. What You say, what You promise, will happen in Your time and not my time. Please keep my definition of what is possible from interfering with my faith in Your will.

Thank You for fulfilling Your promise of a Savior. Thank You for Jesus and what He did on the cross. Thank You for Your perfect timing. I can forever trust in You.

90

LOOK UP

*"But none says, 'Where is God my Maker,
who gives songs in the night.'"*
JOB 35:10 ESV

God, I'm in a time of darkness and trouble, and I look to You. I pray for comfort in my distress and wisdom in my choices. I come to You with complete sincerity. I'm sorry for the times I haven't come to You with complete belief. Sometimes I get so caught up in the things happening around me, I forget to look up. I get so busy trying to help myself, I forget that You always have a hand extended to me.

I take that hand today, Father. Fill my heart with songs to sing while I wait for Your aid. Instead of looking at my night, I will look to the stars You have placed in my life—the blessings and the people I love. I'm confident that when I turn to You, I will find that no matter what happens, everything will be okay.

91

BELIEVE IN JESUS

And who can win this battle against the world?
Only those who believe that Jesus is the Son of God.
1 JOHN 5:5 NLT

Father, I proclaim today that Jesus is the Son of God. I know that He lived life as one of us and suffered greatly under the hands of the people He wanted to save. I believe that He died on the cross for my sins and was laid to rest in a tomb. Then three days later, He rose and defeated death for all of us. Now that I have accepted Him into my heart, I am a new woman, bathed in the blood, bought with a price.

Because of this confidence in Jesus, I will overcome the world. Thank You, God, that I have nothing to fear. Let me find joy in the things that seem hard. Let me find peace where others see chaos. When death comes near, let me rejoice in the eternal life You offer. Thank You!

92

DO IT RIGHT

Trust in the LORD and do good;
dwell in the land and enjoy safe pasture.
PSALM 37:3 NIV

Lord, it seems like those who do wrong are the ones progressing in life. I feel like I'm doing everything right, following Your ways, but am still so far behind. Help me to remember that You know our hearts. In the end, You will be the One to cast judgments on character, not on our achievements in this world.

Open my eyes to where I am needed. Allow my heart to focus on being good. Give me peace so I'm content where I am. If I'm always looking to be somewhere else, I might miss what I can do for You where I'm at.

Doing it the right way may take longer and may be harder, but in the long run, You promise me it will all be worth it.

PEACE OF MIND

"I am leaving you with a gift—peace of mind and heart. And the peace I give is a gift the world cannot give. So don't be troubled or afraid."

JOHN 14:27 NLT

This life can be so crazy, Lord. I can try to control it as much as I can, but in the end, You are the only one in control. You ask me to rely on You during stressful situations, and in return, I am gifted with a peace that surpasses all understanding. If I look for that same peace of mind anywhere else in this world, I won't be able to find it.

People don't understand it, God! When I fully access this peace, I can be perceived as if I don't care. But You and I know better. I care about He who brings all things, not the circumstances themselves. I'm confident—no matter what—everything will work together for my good because I love You. And more importantly, You love me. Thank You!

94

KINDNESS PREVAILS

*And the Lord's servant must not
be quarrelsome but kind to everyone,
able to teach, patiently enduring evil.*
2 TIMOTHY 2:24 ESV

God, how can I be kind to those around me today? In what ways can I spread Your love? Let me teach others who You are through what I do and say. It can be tempting to ignore those around me or lash out when I'm angry. I'm sometimes even afraid to become involved with others because I'm scared I could get hurt or make their problems worse.

But You know what amazing things happen when I choose kindness. I won't fight for the last word or seek payback on those who have done me wrong. Point me to the places in my life where I am being petty, selfish, or mean for no reason. Those things have no place in Your kingdom. Kindness will be harder some days, but love always prevails.

95

STAND FIRM

*"Everyone will hate you because of me, but the
one who stands firm to the end will be saved."*
MARK 13:13 NIV

Lord, You tell me that I will be persecuted for what I
believe. I'm scared for that to happen, but I trust in
You with every fiber of my being. When the time comes,
give me the strength to stand firm for You. Grant me the
right words to speak and the wisdom to act.

When things become hard, God, I am confident
that You will come for me, promising that if I stick by
You, I'll be saved—maybe not from my circumstances
but from a spiritual death. Help me to find peace and
joy in that, Father.

Your Son has overcome the world. In His name,
there is no fear. When the day comes to show I'm a
Christ follower, I hope I will proudly declare I am Yours.

96

FLAWLESS

"Before I formed you in the womb I knew you,
and before you were born I consecrated you;
I appointed you a prophet to the nations."
JEREMIAH 1:5 ESV

Lord, thank You for reminding me daily that I have always been and always will be a part of Your plan. I was designed thoughtfully by You, the Creator of the skies. Every personality trait, every dream on my heart, even the way I look was crafted perfectly Your way.

There are some days when I don't like certain parts of me. I wish I could change them to meet the world's standards. But You, Father, proclaim that we are not of this world. We were never meant to fit in. Every part of our personality was made for a specific plan for Your will. Not for my family, friends, or those around me. Not even me. For You!

Let me be confident in that truth today. I am flawless in You.

97

DEAD TO SIN

So you also should consider yourselves
to be dead to the power of sin and
alive to God through Christ Jesus.
ROMANS 6:11 NLT

God, thank You for letting me know that once I've given my heart to You and have fully accepted Your will, I will no longer have to worry about the sin of my past. I am forgiven and new. For everything I need, I will look to You.

Let me think the same for those who have done wrong but are now fully embracing a life in You. It can be hard to forget the past, but I will fasten my gaze forward. If You have forgiven them, Father, I will do my best to do the same. We are all made new in the power of Jesus Christ.

Make Your presence known to Your children so we can all become alive in You.

98

FULLY

*"Indeed, the very hairs of your head are all
numbered. Don't be afraid; you are
worth more than many sparrows."*
LUKE 12:7 NIV

God, I could spend a lifetime looking for someone who knows every little thing about me and loves me anyway. This includes someone accepting not only the best parts but my ugly bits. The times when I'm mean and selfish. The moments I'm angry and my enemies get the best of me.

You know all the details about me, Father. I'm fully known and understood by You. That could scare me, but You tell me that You fully love me too. This is an assurance that I can come to You every day as I am, and there won't ever be judgment or shame cast on me.

I'm sorry if I ever take Your presence for granted. Instead of trying to satisfy this longing for acceptance in the world, I will find it fully in You.

GOD HAS AUTHORITY

*Jesus came and said to them, "All authority
in heaven and on earth has been given to me."*
MATTHEW 28:18 ESV

Lord, help me to understand that You are completely sovereign. In the good times and the bad, You are in control. When I need help, I will look to You before anyone else. Because of this, I can be confident that what happens to me will be turned and used for Your good.

When my life feels out of control, the enemy tells me that You don't care, that You have given no meaning to me, that You have no power on earth. Help me fight those voices and tell them they are wrong.

You have full authority, God. Thank You for promising to come back for us when the time is right. You have won every battle against the darkness and will win many more. Help me fight for You and accept Your authority in my life.

100

A SERVANT'S HEART

Mary responded, "I am the Lord's servant.
May everything you have said about me
come true." And then the angel left her.
LUKE 1:38 NLT

Father, let me put aside what I want to become Your servant. If I'm standing in the way of Your will, I pray that You will guide my steps. Where should I go? What should I do?

I want what You say to come true for me, Lord, even if I don't understand. If You give me what I desire, thank You. But if You have other plans, I will lay aside what I want. Give me a heart like Mary's, open and yearning to live for You.

Your will is perfect. Your will is good. Like Your Son, who was a servant to His disciples, let me actively serve those You have brought into my life and do the things You ask of me.

101

MY DEFENDER

*Though an army besiege me, my heart will
not fear; though war break out against
me, even then I will be confident.*
PSALM 27:3 NIV

God, I sometimes feel at war with the world around me. Where I seek acceptance, I find isolation. Instead of love, I see hate. Every opposition I face, the enemy uses to pull me away from You. Hurtful words, broken hearts, and uncontrollable anxiety are thrown my way, and it takes all my strength to defend against them.

I will not falter in fear, Lord. I ask You to fight for me. Go before me toward my adversaries.

Thank You that I don't have to fight these battles on my own. When people—or even my own thoughts—come at me with intentions to hurt, I don't have to be afraid. I can find confidence in the fact that You will always fight for me. You are and will be my defender.

102

QUIETLY CONFIDENT

And this righteousness will bring peace.
Yes, it will bring quietness and confidence forever.
ISAIAH 32:17 NLT

Help me to remember that my confidence in You doesn't have to be loud and intense, Lord. While You long for us to shout Your praises, I also believe in Your way and not the world's. Jesus came quietly. A carpenter instead of a king. In a manger instead of in a palace. Appearing to shepherds instead of soldiers.

Others may see confidence as forceful and bold, overworked and deafening. But You show us a confidence that's quiet and peaceful, bold in trust for something bigger than all of this.

Miracles still happen today. Sometimes in the most quiet and simple ways. Let me trust that today, God. If I choose Your righteousness, I have access to a peace more powerful than armies. Though it may not look like what the world gives, I can be sure it is far better.

103

MY SALVATION

"Surely God is my salvation; I will trust and not be afraid. The Lord, the Lord himself, is my strength and my defense; he has become my salvation."

<small>ISAIAH 12:2 NIV</small>

Jesus is the only one true way to salvation. It doesn't matter how many church meetings I attend, or how much money I have, or the good deeds I perform. The only reason I have salvation is because Jesus loved me enough to die for me. If I accept Him into my heart as my rightful Savior, I know I will be with You in heaven.

I don't have to be afraid of earthly circumstances or rely on my own strength to push through my days. I don't have to worry that my missteps and stumbles in sin will prevent me from my eternal life with You.

Thank You, Jesus, for taking my sins and dying on the cross for me. I never have to earn my own salvation. I can just live in You.

104

THE ARMOR

Therefore take up the whole armor of God,
that you may be able to withstand in the
evil day, and having done all, to stand firm.
EPHESIANS 6:13 ESV

Thank You, God, for gifting us with armor that we can use to fight our battles: the belt of truth, the breastplate of righteousness, the shield of faith, the helmet of salvation, and the sword of the Spirit. I know, Lord, that once we choose You, we are at war with the enemy. It's not always a physical battle but one of spiritual warfare. These tools are available to me at all times and will calm me, grant me wisdom, and strengthen my courage.

You have given me everything I need for my calling. Empower me to stand strong when the day to fight comes. Allow me to be courageous and fearless, following the ultimate example of Jesus. With this armor, I will stand firm for You.

105

LIGHT OF MY LIFE

In him was life, and that life was
the light of all mankind.
JOHN 1:4 NIV

*L*ord, I choose to believe today that Your Son is the true light for this world. While I was lost in darkness, it was His goodness that led me out. When this life is hard to live and I get hurt because of its brokenness, I will still find joy in my Savior. My life starts and ends in Him. Because of His sacrifice, there will be a day when there is no more heartache or pain.

I long for that day, Lord, when Jesus comes back to rescue us all again. And I am confident that He will return like He promised. Until then I will do my best to confidently share the light of Christ with all those around me in my words and actions.

106

JESUS IS

Simon Peter answered, "You are the
Messiah, the Son of the living God."
MATTHEW 16:16 NLT

Jesus, You are truly the Son of God who still reigns today. So many people have different names for You and describe You in different ways, but I know that Your Word tells us You came to set captives of sin free. You came to start a new way of life. Now I can go straight to You in a single breath with words of concern or songs of praise. Thank You for breaking down the barrier that once separated us from You.

Even the disciples who lived every day with You had trouble understanding what You were meant to do. But I'm able to see the whole story. I don't even have all the words to describe Your greatness but these: You are who You say You are. And I will proclaim that beautiful name as my everything until we see each other face-to-face.

107

TINY FAITH

"You don't have enough faith," Jesus told them. "I tell you the truth, if you had faith even as small as a mustard seed, you could say to this mountain, 'Move from here to there,' and it would move. Nothing would be impossible."

<small>MATTHEW 17:20 NLT</small>

*L*ord, thank You for being You. Your plans aren't hindered by my humanness. When my faith shakes because of my current circumstances, I know that it won't affect Your will. You are powerful and limitless. While You long for me to be a part of Your plans, I don't define them. But I do want in. Give me the courage.

Let me access the faith that moves mountains, God. I know that the Holy Spirit in me is the same One that was with Jesus in the tomb, the same One with Paul on his missions. Even the tiniest bit of faith will do the greatest things.

108

MORE THAN

"I want you to show love, not offer sacrifices. I want you to know me more than I want burnt offerings."
<small>HOSEA 6:6 NLT</small>

Lord, I crave Your presence more than I crave time in church. I want Your truth and guidance more than I want religion. I desire heart-to-heart prayers rather than scripted spiritual practices. If I do any of these things because I need to check off a box for the week, without a focus on You, they mean nothing. They do nothing to refill my life or honor You. I can say I'm a Christian, but does it mean anything if I don't have a real relationship with You?

Father, You are more than a building. You are so much more than the rules this world and broken people have placed on Your children. Open my eyes to the parts of my life where I care more about performance than being Yours. Lead me to a life of fuller devotion to You.

109

MY SHEPHERD

The LORD is my shepherd, I lack nothing.
PSALM 23:1 NIV

Lord, thank You for meeting me where I am. Thank You for supplying everything I need right now. Thank You for this moment with You. Like a shepherd tending to his sheep, You guide me in the right direction, protect me from outside forces, and steer me away from paths that could lead to pain. Even when I don't understand what's happening, I will forever trust that You know best. I will trust that You will craft all circumstances for my sake, according to Your will, which is always perfect and always good.

If I am lacking anything, God, let me fill up that emptiness with You. When I am angry about what I don't have, remind me that all I need is You. All the things of this life I will leave behind, but I will never stray far from Your loving hands and Your promise of forever.

110

BRIGHTEST MORNINGS

"If you pour yourself out for the hungry and satisfy the desire of the afflicted, then shall your light rise in the darkness and your gloom be as the noonday."
ISAIAH 58:10 ESV

I want to follow where You lead, God. Who do You want me to help? Whom should I share Your light with today? For if I do good things in Your name, You promise that I will shine in darkness, stand out against hate. All of it will be a reflection of who You are.

This world sometimes makes me think that I have to look out for myself and no one else. But You don't ask that of me, Father. You tell me to pour out myself for those in need. You ask me to wash feet. Sometimes the best way to deal with my own problems is to help someone else with theirs.

Turn my eyes on what You would want me to do for others. For the darkest nights become the brightest mornings when I help others and show them Your light.

111

WHAT I REAP

Do not be deceived: God cannot be mocked.
A man reaps what he sows.
GALATIANS 6:7 NIV

I know, God, that I will never fool You like I sometimes fool those around me. You know my heart when I say I'm fine but I'm not; You know the truth when I lie to make myself look good in front of others. Lord, I'm sorry for saying I give all to You but still holding as tightly as ever with both fists to what I want, my plans, my certainty.

Like any situation, I can only ever get out what I put in. If I don't fully trust You with my life, how will You ever be able to show me Your plans? If I don't give over my pain and hurt, how will I ever be able to accept Your healing?

Lord, help me give You everything today, not to reap a plentiful harvest for my own benefit but to reap a beautiful relationship with You.

112

WHEN I FEEL LONELY

*The Lord keeps watch over you as you
come and go, both now and forever.*
Psalm 121:8 nlt

*L*ord, I've heard the common saying that I meet people for a season, a reason, or a lifetime. Thank You, Lord, that You apply to all of these times and more. You're present in every season. Instead of just a reason, You are the purpose of my life. And I don't just get You for a lifetime. I get You forever.

When I feel lonely, You are near. You never leave me. Even Jesus understands the depths of loneliness when He walked this life. When I cry out, You get it. Thank You, Father. I can be confident that when I feel alone, it's temporary. My feelings are real but are a result of this broken world, not because of the absence of my heavenly protector.

You are here and watching out for me. Let me rest in that peace and protection today.

DENYING

And the Lord turned and looked at Peter.
And Peter remembered the saying of the Lord,
how he had said to him, "Before the rooster
crows today, you will deny me three times."
LUKE 22:61 ESV

Father, I say I would never be like Peter and deny You. But Peter only did it three times before he remembered his promise. I can't count the times I have chosen my comfort over Your ways. When I choose hate, when I choose bitterness or anger, resentment, or my superiority to others, I'm denying Jesus' name. When I allow bullying to persist or injustice to exist, I am not following Your will.

So many people pull away from the church and You because of the ways some Christians act. Lord, please let me be a light that draws people to the flame of Your love. I don't want to push away others because of the heat of my own desires or brokenness. Let me confidently show them You.

114

YES! AMEN!

For no matter how many promises God has made,
they are "Yes" in Christ. And so through him the
"Amen" is spoken by us to the glory of God.
2 CORINTHIANS 1:20 NIV

Thank You, God, that all Your promises throughout the Old Testament were answered by Jesus. In this way, He is the answer to all my questions, all my needs. You have given me Your Word to study, and I understand that what You say is true. Thank You, Lord, that because of the holy sacrifice given to us, I can now be in constant communication with You.

Help me to be confident like Christ. I want to have the boundless trust to follow where You lead. When I am scared to step into the plans You have for me, fill me instead with power to shout "Amen!" While Jesus was Your "yes" to my cry for a Savior, let me answer "yes" to the offer of Your will in my life.

115

TEARS TO SPRINGS

When they walk through the Valley of Weeping,
it will become a place of refreshing springs.
The autumn rains will clothe it with blessings.
PSALM 84:6 NLT

*L*ord, thank You for being there during the hard moments of my life. I don't understand why certain things happen, but I do know that You make all things good. Give me the strength to view tears as cleaning springs. Allow me the peace to trust You through the pain and ache, knowing that I'm becoming more like Christ with every heartbeat.

This doesn't make it easy, Father, and I ask for Your loving arms to hold me and my loved ones during hardships. I will never know why things happen, Lord, but in the end, You'll have the last word. There will be no more tears, or hate, or death. I will wait for You and that day with worship and praise on my lips. You will make everything right in time.

TO BE HEALED

He said to her, "Daughter, your faith has made
you well. Go in peace. Your suffering is over."
MARK 5:34 NLT

*L*ord, I sometimes feel like the woman with the affliction, constantly seeking the edge of Your robe for healing from sickness, from heartache, and from sin. But Jesus doesn't tell her only His power has healed her; He says that her faith has made her well. She believed with all her heart that just one touch would satisfy her need.

God, I want to have faith like she had. Faith that no matter what happens, You have unbreakable power. Confidence that You still answer prayers. That power in You is also in me because of Your gift of the Holy Spirit. Let me find that belief today, Father. The belief that whatever may come my way, You are in complete control of it.

At the end of all of this, You have promised me the end of suffering in eternity with You. Thank You, Jesus.

117

NOT EASY

He said: "LORD, the God of Israel, there is no God like you in heaven or on earth—you who keep your covenant of love with your servants who continue wholeheartedly in your way."

2 CHRONICLES 6:14 NIV

✻

Father, there's nothing in my life that matches Your greatness. The people and things that give me temporary pleasure are no match to what You feed my soul. You are powerful and steadfast. Above that, You love Your children and have kept a vow with us through the ages. You promise me that if I stick to Your ways, follow Your path, You'll prepare a home for me in heaven. You will continue to pour out love on me.

Your way on earth for me isn't easy, and there are days when I don't feel You are near; but I know one day, there will be no separation between us. I can't wait for that day!

118

WHEN I AM BULLIED

See what kind of love the Father has given to us,
that we should be called children of God; and so
we are. The reason why the world does not
know us is that it did not know him.

1 JOHN 3:1 ESV

Lord, thank You for reminding me that I am a child of a king. I am not worthless, stupid, ugly, or any other untrue and unkind word. I was bought with a price paid by Jesus, my Savior. I don't deserve to be treated with disrespect or unkindness by others because I have so much value to the kingdom of heaven. I am seen as deserving of love and dignity by my Creator.

When I am being treated poorly, give me the patience to stay calm, the courage to speak up for myself, and Your love to show those who bully there is another way to live. It may be hard, but You, God, will always give me strength.

119

AWESOME GOD

*"How great you are, O Sovereign LORD!
There is no one like you. We have never
even heard of another God like you!"*

2 SAMUEL 7:22 NLT

You are awesome, God! I want to thank You for the amazing things You do and take the time today to proclaim Your wonderful nature. There's nothing in this world that compares to You. You are full of grace, mercy, and peace. You still perform miracles. Your hand is still at work in this world. You make Yourself known.

Give me opportunities to share this news with those I meet. Grant me the words and wisdom to know whom You have put in my path and when I should speak. Everyone deserves to hear the glorious message of Christ; we all deserve to be told how much we're loved by our heavenly Father.

I am confident, Lord, in Your greatness. Thank You for always showing me who You are when I choose to look.

120

SPEAK MY NAME

Jesus said to her, "Mary." She turned
toward him and cried out in Aramaic,
"Rabboni!" (which means "Teacher").
JOHN 20:16 NIV

I can't imagine the darkness Mary had faced before meeting Jesus. For her, Jesus may have been the only safe haven from memories too painful to carry alone. I can also be ashamed of who I was before Christ. When Jesus was buried, I'm sure Mary felt that all hope was lost.

How many times have I been there, Lord? How many times has the devil reminded me who I was?

But thank You, Father, that I know the end of the story. Thank You that Jesus defeated death, rose again, and met Mary in the garden, speaking her name. Speak my name. I don't have to feel guilty for who I was because I'm a whole new being in You from the moment You called me by name.

I will live that truth today for myself and others.

121

DOING THE WORK

After all, who is Apollos? Who is Paul? We are only God's servants through whom you believed the Good News. Each of us did the work the Lord gave us.

1 Corinthians 3:5 NLT

Father, what would You ask me to do today? I want to be open to situations in my life that need my talents, my eyes, my heart. You've created me with the chance to follow in my Savior's footsteps and become a servant for those around me.

My talents come from You. My heart beats for what Yours beats for. My eyes cry at what makes You cry, God. When I come to my end, I want Jesus to say that I've been a good, faithful servant.

So, let me do the work, Lord, even if it's hard, because I know my willingness and my strength is from You. I believe in Jesus and what He did, and I'll try passionately to reveal You in everything I do.

122

ALWAYS

Rejoice always, pray without ceasing,
give thanks in all circumstances; for this
is the will of God in Christ Jesus for you.
1 THESSALONIANS 5:16–18 ESV

Lord, forgive me for adding my own endings to Your commandments for me. I need to rejoice at all times not just when something goes my way. I have to pray without ceasing even when I'm getting frustrated with the answers. I must give thanks in *all* seasons.

That can be so hard when this world is telling me what my life should look like. However, You want me to ask what You want for my life not what the world wants.

So, today I praise Your name. I will continue to pray until You choose to answer. And I thank You for everything I have in my life, because all good things are blessings from above. Thank You that I can always be confident in my God.

123

TAKE REFUGE

Lord my God, I take refuge in you;
save and deliver me from all who pursue me.
PSALM 7:1 NIV

God, sometimes I feel like I'm on the run. From past mistakes and guilt. From anger, sadness, and anxiety. And there are some days when the chase is physical. I find myself needing to stay away from someone, a certain place, or a harmful thing in my life. How can I be confident in You when I feel like the enemy is telling me I'm running scared?

I know, Father, that the enemy is spouting lies. Instead of running away, I'm running to take refuge in You. I may be seen as weak to the world, but I am strong and saved in You.

Fight those who want me to falter and fall, the things trying to pull me away from You. I know that I am forever safe in Your arms.

124

PRAY FOR LEADERS

First of all, then, I urge that supplications, prayers,
intercessions, and thanksgivings be made for all people, for
kings and all who are in high positions, that we may lead a
peaceful and quiet life, godly and dignified in every way.
1 Timothy 2:1–2 esv

God, give me wisdom to choose the right leader for my nation and my home. I want what is best for future generations, my loved ones, and the kids in my life. Bring someone to the forefront with a longing for Your heart and Your way in the world.

I know, Lord, that You're fully in control and aware of who is chosen and how they will act. When situations look dim, remind me that You have the final say, and Your holy judgment will shine a light on the truth.

I pray for righteous leaders, and I'm thankful for the ones already working, trying to do Your work. I pray that we all choose Your love above all.

125

TRUE WISDOM

"To God belong wisdom and power;
counsel and understanding are his."
JOB 12:13 NIV

God, You are the source of true and pure wisdom. Thank You for the people in my life whom I trust and the times You spoke through them. Christian media resources can help me greatly and point me to Your ways, but nothing will compare to sitting in Your presence and seeking Your voice.

I'm sorry for the times I chose those things first, but You are still full of grace and blessings when You use those things to point me in the right direction. You long for connection and conversation with me, and I was created with a missing piece only You can give.

When I need help and advice, please speak openly to me, Lord. I crave Your counsel above what I want. Give me Your wisdom and power to make choices pleasing to You, and give me understanding and peace when I come to an answer in situations I face.

126

MY TREASURE

*"Wherever your treasure is,
there the desires of your heart will also be."*
MATTHEW 6:21 NLT

Father, don't let me get caught up in the things of this world. I don't want to always be focused on how much money I make, how big my house is, and how much stuff I have in it. When I'm focused on those things, I miss out on the countless blessings that are priceless.

Thank You, God, for my family and friends. Thank You for the honest work I get to do daily because of the body You gave me. Thank You for the body You gave me! Let me focus on the good and true things, the ones that show who You are.

My treasure ultimately should be in You. Everything else will sometimes disappoint me, but You'll always come through for me. Amen!

127

BECOMING WHOLE

In Christ you have been brought to fullness.
He is the head over every power and authority.
COLOSSIANS 2:10 NIV

Lord, I'm tired of fighting every day to be accepted. I'm done with proving to others I'm significant. The more I try, the emptier I feel and the further I am from being happy. As long as I use the measurements of this world, I'll never feel like enough.

But if I turn to Jesus and what He has done for me, I will be full beyond measure with acceptance. I am worth more than I could ever imagine. And in that truth, I'm whole. I can find meaning and purpose.

Thank You for being in control. Thank You for always showing us that power. I can rely on You for every single need.

128

HIS GRACE

*Grace to all who love our Lord Jesus
Christ with an undying love.*
EPHESIANS 6:24 NIV

Thank You, God, for offering me grace at all times. Even if I don't accept it one day, I can find it the next. If I take Your grace and slip into sin, You still love me and offer me grace again and again. No matter what I've done, I'm never too far from Your loving acceptance.

I will hang on to that truth as hard as I can. I'm sorry for the moments when I don't accept Your grace and turn from You to follow my own pursuits. Light a fire in me to always pursue Your will and to desire what You want above what I want.

I love You, Lord. I'm sorry my love is messy. Teach me to love like Jesus—with the patience, kindness, and grace that You give me every single day.

129

PRESERVE ME

Though I walk in the midst of trouble,
you preserve my life.
PSALM 138:7 ESV

*L*ord, there are so many things I try to keep in pristine condition: my relationships with others, items from my past, money in my savings account, even my skin and hair. But these things will fail me. Everything changes. If I rely too heavily on them, I may end up hurt. While I try to save these things, they will not save me.

You're the only One who can preserve me. Jesus is who I hope for and need every moment of the day. While most of this earth will fade away, You will still be constant. If I look to You in times of trouble, I know You will be there no matter what. You constantly save me, Father, from the enemy and myself. Thank You for loving endlessly.

130

GOD'S VOICE

God said, "Let there be light,"
and there was light.
GENESIS 1:3 NIV

*L*ord, the power of Your voice is inexplicable. In the beginning, You spoke into the vast emptiness of the world and saw what it could be with Your craftsmanship. Four simple words pulled light from darkness, created greatness from nothing. No other voice can stand against its majesty.

I'm constantly surrounded by voices, Father. Some are trustworthy. Some aren't. I hear physical voices from friends, family, bosses, and media. And sometimes I'm deafened by the voices from my past, my own voice in my head.

Help me to always seek Your voice among the others. When I find it, I also find power to speak out against fear. I find peace in the middle of chaos. I find meaning in You when there is none in the world. Let me know when I hear You, God. I'll trust Your voice today and follow where You lead.

131

CREATOR KNOWS BEST

My help comes from the LORD,
the Maker of heaven and earth.
PSALM 121:2 NIV

*L*ord, I need Your help! I'm burnt out and still seek-ing guidance. I'm sorry for going to other methods of coping before coming to You. I think deep down I thought it would be easier to deal with my problems by myself rather than following Your way. Thank You once again for Your endless grace and understanding when it comes to my humanness.

God, I trust that Your help will be what I need, because You know best. You not only formed me, You created the world I live in, how it works and everything in it. What I bring to You isn't new. You have already accorded it with Your will before I even ask.

Please give me the patience with myself and the confidence to follow in Your footsteps by choosing to use my uncomfortable circumstances for my good. I'm becoming the woman You want me to be.

132

HIS WORD

"Is not my word like fire, declares the LORD,
and like a hammer that breaks the rock in pieces?"
JEREMIAH 23:29 ESV

I can't hide from You, God. You know my heart better than anyone else. I come to You humble and in awe of Your great forgiveness.

Thank You for Your Word, which is truly like fire. With each reading, it exposes my wrongdoings. It shows how I can be more like Jesus in every way. Let this fire burn up the darkness in me. Lord, purify me from sin, harden parts of me to grow stronger in faith, and soften pieces of me to love purely.

And I want to thank You for using Your Word like a hammer. You broke open my hard heart, and now it cries for what makes You cry. You challenge me to be a better servant, follower, and friend. Never stop letting Your Word affect and mold me as long as I live.

133

ULTIMATE HEALING

Jesus said, "I will come and heal him."
MATTHEW 8:7 NLT

ord, thank You for Jesus' time on earth. Everything He did was for my ultimate healing. I will eventually spend eternity with Him, free of pain and suffering, full of joy and blessings. That can be hard to remember in this life.

We weren't created to live a life of physical pain, but because of the world's brokenness, my loved ones and I must face it daily. Thank You for the miracles You have provided over the years. And thank You, God, for the times that healing meant my loved ones went to be with You. Though losing them was difficult, I trust that I will see them again one day.

Remind me that Jesus' healing may not cover every physical ailment, but it always heals us spiritually. Once we accept Him as our Savior, our souls are restored and made clean in His name, a healing we can't accomplish ourselves. Thank You, Jesus!

134

TRUST HIS HELP

"O our God, won't you stop them? We are powerless against this mighty army that is about to attack us. We do not know what to do, but we are looking to you for help."

2 CHRONICLES 20:12 NLT

In times of trouble, Lord, my way of doing things may be strange to those who don't know You. Instead of tirelessly searching for things to do or preparing for what will happen next, I stay still. I seek Your will. I feel powerless against this incoming storm, but I know the wind and the rain cease at the sound of Your voice.

I look to You for my needs. You're aware of what I'm going through. Not one of my tears has slipped through unnoticed by You. I'll trust Your timing, and You will deliver me. Maybe it won't be in the way I am expecting, but it will be good just the same. I'll use this time to strengthen my faith in You.

135

BE READY

"You also must be ready, because the Son of Man will come at an hour when you do not expect him."
Luke 12:40 niv

Jesus, I'm waiting for Your return. You promised one day to come back for me, and I believe that promise. Your timing is always perfect. You're never too early or too late. I'll trust in that. Even when I think my life is out of control, I can see it as a reminder that my place is not of this world but in heaven. Everything will make sense once I step through those gates. And soon You will be coming back to take us to the home You've prepared for us.

Let me be ready, Lord. Allow me to love the present but live as though You're returning today. I don't ever want to become so caught up with the things of this life that I would rather stay than go. I am so excited to see Your face.

136

FIGHTING WORDS

He made my mouth like a sharp sword; in the shadow of his hand he hid me; he made me a polished arrow; in his quiver he hid me away.
ISAIAH 49:2 ESV

Lord, I'm a soldier in Your army, called to fight for Your name. One way I can defend You is with my voice. It's so important. You ask me to speak out against hate and injustice. You tell me to defend the poor, hungry, and lost. I'm supposed to be a voice for the voiceless. Give me courage and wisdom for this.

My words are a mighty sword. They pierce and fight. They protect and defend. But they can also harm if I'm not careful. Let Your love and truth be behind everything I say.

I'm an arrow for Christ. I'm forceful and great. I'm hidden and protected by my Savior until the perfect time. I will trust the power You have given me and use it to fight for You.

SETTLE MY HEART

*"There is only one thing worth being
concerned about. Mary has discovered it,
and it will not be taken away from her."*
Luke 10:42 nlt

God, I always thought Mary's sister, Martha, got a bad rap. Mary was praised while Martha was corrected. I thought the older sister was just trying to serve her guests as well as she could. But I understand when I dig deeper into scripture, she was letting what she wanted to do for Jesus interfere with what Jesus wanted for her.

How many times have I done that, Father? Went through motions without meaning. I do so many things in Your name but don't stop to know if they are the right things. I'm sorry.

Lord, settle my heart, and let me sit in Your presence. That's what You and I crave most of all. Remind me that sometimes You don't ask me to work but to stay still to feel Your companionship.

138

HE SEES ME

She gave this name to the Lord who spoke to her:
"You are the God who sees me," for she said,
"I have now seen the One who sees me."
GENESIS 16:13 NIV

Thank You, God, for always having Your eyes on me. Even when I stray from Your path, You're still looking out for me. You're a heavenly Father who sees Your children and cares. But You won't be rushed into Your promises or change them once Your Word is established.

Hagar's child wasn't supposed to be a part of the design for Your people. And while it led to heartache for those involved, You still loved Hagar and her son. You chased after her when she ran like a shepherd following a runaway lamb. You saw her and spoke to her, and because of that, she returned amazed and sure of Your presence.

Fill me with that today, Lord. Thank You for always seeing me and showing me I'm never alone.

139

THE PROTECTOR

For I can do everything through
Christ, who gives me strength.
PHILIPPIANS 4:13 NLT

Lord, there are so many things to worry about. I wake up feeling like I have to brace myself against things I would never have guessed I'd be facing. The news and social media are always bombarding me with negativity and violence, and some days I don't want myself or my loved ones leaving the house.

But You ask me to face the day with You by my side. You have immeasurable power. You can do anything. All I need to do is pray for You to come to my aid. Today, God, I choose to be content.

I am confident that You will provide all my needs. I don't need to fall prey to my anxiety or fear because I know You're the great Protector. Thank You for taking care of me and my loved ones. Please keep giving me Your strength.

140

IMPERFECT VISION

*For now we see in a mirror dimly, but then face
to face. Now I know in part; then I shall know
fully, even as I have been fully known.*
1 Corinthians 13:12 esv

Lord, I know that my view of the world is imperfect.
When You crafted Your creation, it wasn't meant to
be broken. Adam, Eve, and Eden were made perfect, and
You said they were good. But once sin entered the world,
everything shattered. My view and knowledge of You,
of everything, are now blurry and skewed.

But thank You, Jesus, for promising to make all
things clear one day. I may never have the same vision as
You, but I will get the chance to know You as fully as I
can, and I can't wait for that moment.

You know me deeply, all my faults, and still love me.
Thank You for that sacrificial and agape love I will hope-
fully understand at the end. I will still seek Your truth
until then.

141

SEEKING AND KNOCKING

"For everyone who asks receives; the one who seeks finds;
and to the one who knocks, the door will be opened."
MATTHEW 7:8 NIV

God, I ask You now to make a way for me. I have been seeking Your face and Your will. I feel like this is the next step in living the life You created for me. Please place Your hand in this, and I'll work my best to do everything for You. I feel desperate, Lord, for something to finally work right in my life.

But even if this doesn't come through, I will trust in You. My value isn't in what I can provide. My true worth is found in the One who provides all. I'm sorry if I have let other things get in the way of my growing relationship with You. Thank You for never being absent when I'm in need.

142

UNDER GOD'S AUTHORITY

The wife does not have authority over her own
body but yields it to her husband. In the same
way, the husband does not have authority
over his own body but yields it to his wife.
1 CORINTHIANS 7:4 NIV

*L*ord, help me to remember that above being with my husband, my body belongs to You. No matter what I've done or what has happened to me in the past, I am brand-new and wiped clean in the eyes of Jesus. Thank You for letting me share this glorious gift with someone else.

Let me look at my beloved the way You do. Your goodness allows me to have humility, patience, and kindness. I can give my body to my spouse in ways that bless, please, and fulfill him. I also get the chance to receive his body in return. By putting You first, I don't have to worry about issues of authority. Under You, we can both choose to be servants.

143

A COVENANT

But now we have been released from the law, for we died to it and are no longer captive to its power. Now we can serve God, not in the old way of obeying the letter of the law, but in the new way of living in the Spirit.
ROMANS 7:6 NLT

Thank You, Father, that I'm now under a covenant of grace and not a covenant of works. Jesus' sacrifice tore the veil between us and left behind a Helper and Friend in the Holy Spirit. I get to communicate openly with You every day.

If I try to obey the law without Jesus, I will always come up short. But I can pray confidently with power from the Spirit. What more do I need, God? I thank You again and again for all You have done for me, though I don't deserve it. I am redeemed and delivered in Jesus' name alone. Amen!

144

WHEN I FEEL LIKE
I DON'T MATTER

Jesus looked at him and loved him.
MARK 10:21 NIV

God, there are some days when I feel like nobody is truly seeing me. Harsh words and hurt feelings make me want to stay silent and stay at home. It pains me, Lord, and makes me question if I even matter to anybody. It makes me wonder if there is something wrong with me.

Whenever I feel this way, remind me that I matter so much to You. You forever see me, look for me, and always love me. Even as I feel alone, I know You are near, embracing me and covering me in Your love. When I am hurt by others, give me the strength to give grace in those situations instead of bitterness.

Correct me in Your way so I can continue becoming the woman You created me to be. I am priceless and full of value as I'm one of Your daughters. I will receive and live that. Amen.

145

TRANQUILITY

A tranquil heart gives life to the flesh,
but envy makes the bones rot.
PROVERBS 14:30 ESV

*L*ord, I've seen what rot can do to things. Mighty trees that reach the sky fall. Structures that were once sound and strong rust and fail. You tell me that what infection can do to Your creation is what envy can do to Your children. It can slowly ruin me before I even know something is wrong, destroying happiness, peace, and—worst of all—my relationship with You.

I can't be confident of how You made me if I'm too busy looking at what others have that I don't. So, God, I ask You to give me a calm heart. I crave the tranquility and understanding that You give about my circumstances and blessings.

When I feel envy building, I'll remember the good things in my life that You provided. As I do this, my heart will give life instead of taking it.

146

WHAT COMES NEXT?

"Then if my people who are called by my name will humble themselves and pray and seek my face and turn from their wicked ways, I will hear from heaven and will forgive their sins and restore their land."
2 CHRONICLES 7:14 NLT

God, I'm so glad that Your goodness doesn't wait for my faithfulness. After I've sinned and I return to You, You are there to take me again into Your arms. You restore me to where I'm supposed to be. You have always cared more about Your children's character than their comfort. I know I'll have to deal with the consequences of my sin, but You will be beside me.

What should I do now, Lord? Trying to understand Your ways isn't what You want. You ask us to practice faith, be humble, and grow in relationship with You. You have forgiven my sins and restored my life. Tell me, Father, what I should do next.

147

DECLARE MY BELIEF

*"Yes, Lord," she replied, "I believe that you are the Messiah,
the Son of God, who is to come into the world."*
JOHN 11:27 NIV

When Martha declared that Jesus was the Messiah, she didn't know her brother was going to be brought back to life. In the midst of heartache and loss and what could be perceived as abandonment from God, she trusts. She holds on to her unshakable and steadfast faith. She says the words out loud that Jesus is still the One sent from God to save the world.

Lord, let me follow in Martha's footsteps, living by faith and not sight. When I'm surrounded by problems and pain, I'll choose to settle in my faith and know that You are a Comforter and a Way-Maker. No matter my circumstances, my confident reply should be that I still believe in You and Your ways. I trust You, God, and I believe one day You will make all things right.

148

STEPPING OUT

As it is written, "I have made you the father of many nations"—in the presence of the God in whom he believed, who gives life to the dead and calls into existence the things that do not exist.

ROMANS 4:17 ESV

Lord, You make the impossible possible. What isn't has no power over what You say is. Thank You for giving me life when I was dead to sin. Thank You for calling me to exist out of numbness and days of simply going through the motions.

Without You, I wouldn't have the faith to live each day fully. I'm willing, Father, to walk through darkness and storms because I know You're with me from beginning to end. Give me the confidence to step boldly into what is in front of me despite my fear. I know You will be there for the first step and all those after.

149

WHEN I CAN'T SLEEP

In peace I will lie down and sleep,
for you alone, O LORD, will keep me safe.
PSALM 4:8 NLT

Father, I haven't even scratched the surface of the meaning of true peace that only You can give. I lie awake some nights, tossing and turning, worrying about this and that. Even as I've given You my circumstances and problems, I still think about what will happen.

Tonight, Lord, I accept that peace. Instead of choosing fear, I hold on to Your safety. I am sure that You are in control. And the more I try to take it back, the more I get in the way of Your will. I'm sorry for not trusting You. Let this assurance pass from me to those around me who are also fighting their own sleepless battles.

Grant me a restful night so that I can try again tomorrow.

150

CONFIDENT PEACE

"Blessed are the peacemakers, for they
will be called children of God."
MATTHEW 5:9 NIV

*L*ord, make me a confident peacemaker in the place You have put me. Where I find Your peace, I can find confidence in myself. I don't have to give in to my fears and insecurities.

This doesn't mean that I force peace on those around me or only seek it for my own well-being. This is a peace that points back to Christ. It is about reconciliation with what I have done wrong and what wrongs have been done to me. It's a focus on the future that You promise and provide.

Peace doesn't have to be only in a single moment. This peace is available to me every hour, whether I'm in need of it or not. Thank You, Father. I receive that peace today as I hand over the situations in my life that are troubling. Let others seek Your peace that they see in me.

151

WHERE YOU ARE

*Then you moved far away and trouble
moved in next door. I need a neighbor.*
PSALM 22:11 MSG

God, I'm sorry for the times I let sin get the best of me. My troubles and the enemy feel closer than ever, which just amplifies my feelings of Your absence. Because of what I've done, I feel like You've left me even though I know Your Word promises that's not true.

I need Your help, Lord. I can't save myself, and the other things in my life won't be able to rescue me the way You can. I know that when the timing is right, You will come to my aid. I need to be still and have faith in You, God; Your ways are just and true.

You didn't move away. You're alive in my heart and are never far from me.

152

THIS JOY

So there was much joy in that city.
ACTS 8:8 ESV

*L*ord, there are so many things in this life that can cause exceeding joy. Health, stability, the reconciliation and forgiveness of close friends, church revival, new believers, love. All of these things are wonderful in Your precious name.

Only You can provide joy that is long-lasting and meaningful. If I am only confident in things on the surface, I'll never truly access what You provide—joy in my salvation. I'm so thankful for Your blessings, but I shouldn't let them come between me and the One who blesses.

Joy isn't about where we are at. This joy is about where we are going.

153

FILL ME UP

Be on guard. Stand firm in the faith.
Be courageous. Be strong.
1 CORINTHIANS 16:13 NLT

God, I try to meditate on all the strengths Jesus displayed. He calmed storms and waves. He healed sickness. Immeasurable power was not only in His body but in the very garments He wore. Let me be confident and sure that the same strength lies in me. I know I can stand today amid any hardship because You are right there with me, holding me up.

I know I've asked for these things before, but I'm human. I know I need to ask You again and again for help. Fill me up with courage. Fill me up with patience to watch You work. While life around me spirals, I know that everything You are is steadfast. I will fasten myself to that truth. Among troubles, I can always look to You for comfort and guidance.

154

CONFIDENCE IN JESUS' SACRIFICE

God demonstrates his own love for us in this:
While we were still sinners, Christ died for us.
ROMANS 5:8 NIV

Lord, I believe that when Jesus died for Your children's sins, I was included. It doesn't matter what I've done; I'm loved and whole in Christ. And this death wasn't finished before I was redeemed; Jesus died while I was still lost in sin. He didn't even wait until I believed. You cared for us so deeply that Your Son, Jesus Christ, gave it all without asking anything in return.

I can't imagine or fully understand that kind of love. I'm confident that even though I'm not able to save myself, *You* can. The moment I accepted Your sacrifice, I gained a heavenly home. Sin and death are broken forever. Thank You, Father!

I'll take this brand-new identity and live a life mirroring the One who saved me. In Jesus' name, amen!

155

WHEN I FEEL LEFT OUT

*The Spirit of GOD, the Master, is on me because
GOD anointed me. He sent me to preach good
news to the poor, heal the heartbroken, announce
freedom to all captives, pardon all prisoners.*
ISAIAH 61:1 MSG

Father, I knew when I chose to follow You that some people in my life would turn their backs on me. I can't serve the world and You, and there is darkness that despises You and Your ways. So, there are times when I'm left out and lonely because of my faith. While my relationship with You is so important, I'm still hurt by how others treat me. Sometimes I even feel different from other Christians.

Thank You, God, that Your Son experienced the same things. He was rejected by those He loved. You know my pain. Heal my broken heart as I confidently step into the freedom You give. I know You have a plan for me. My value is not in others, only in You.

FOLLOWING WHERE HE LEADS

*On that day, when evening had come, he said
to them, "Let us go across to the other side."*
MARK 4:35 ESV

*L*ord, thank You for always guiding me. Sometimes the road is clear and the day is sunny. I'm excited to arrive at my destination. But when evening comes or when fog rolls in, I find it hard to take a single step. Let me listen to the sound of Your sweet voice calling me forward. Let me feel Your presence walking beside me.

I don't have to be afraid of the twists and turns. I can eagerly await the valleys in my life as I look ahead to the hills. I know these valleys can be used to strengthen my spirit and faith. I would never know the amount of trust I have in You if it was never tested.

Even when I see a storm brewing, like the disciples on Jesus' ship, I will follow devotedly to "the other side."

HE PARTS THE SEA

*Then Moses raised his hand over the sea,
and the L ORD opened up a path through the
water with a strong east wind. The wind blew
all that night, turning the seabed into dry land.*
EXODUS 14:21 NLT

Thank You, Father, for continually making a way
for me. When Moses met the sea, He didn't tell
Your people to swim or build boats to make it across.
He awaited Your instruction with patience even as his
enemies drew closer and closer. And at just the right
moment, You parted the water.

I'm sorry for the times I tried to outrun troubles on
my own. I'm sorry for the moments I didn't trust You to
come through. But always at the right time, according
to Your will, You showed me the way to go.

Your wind blows all night until daylight comes; You
keep me dry and safe. All I need to do is trust and be
still.

158

I AM UNDERSTOOD

And the Holy Spirit helps us in our weakness.
For example, we don't know what God wants us
to pray for. But the Holy Spirit prays for us with
groanings that cannot be expressed in words.
ROMANS 8:26 NLT

Father, I'm absolutely secure in Your arms. You never look at me with condemnation, and no matter what I've done, there's no separation from Your love. Because I have called Jesus my Savior, I can live in the Spirit. It is the gorgeous gift You left behind and the promise of Your Son's return.

But that doesn't keep me from suffering in this broken world. It doesn't mean I'm strong all the time. Sometimes, Lord, I'm so weak and sad that I can't find the words to even pray.

But thank You that the Spirit prays for me when I can't. Thank You for understanding me when I don't understand myself. I will always be confident in the truth. You are for me and love me unconditionally.

159

CONFIDENCE IN FAITH

Do not be terrified by them, for the LORD your God,
who is among you, is a great and awesome God.
DEUTERONOMY 7:21 NIV

*L*ord, calm my heart. When I'm anxious, remind me again and again that You're in control. No one has and no one will ever defeat You. You are awesome and powerful!

Please deliver me from my fear and temptations. I know that I can't be threatened by darkness because my Savior has already defeated death and sin. Thank You, God, that I'm covered in that victory. I receive this promise today and know Your power walks beside me every day.

Bless me with the boldness and confidence of unbreakable faith. I don't have to be afraid, because when I face adversity or hardship, You're fighting for me. Other forces will oppose me when they know I'm working for You, but I know the end of the story. I'm victorious in Jesus.

160

MY CONVENIENCE

*"I am the living bread that came down from heaven.
If anyone eats of this bread, he will live forever. And the
bread that I will give for the life of the world is my flesh."*
JOHN 6:51 ESV

Father, there are so many times in the Bible where You meet Your children's physical needs. I'm certain from Your Word that You care about what I have to eat and drink, where I live, and what I do. And You sent Jesus to meet my spiritual needs. You care so much for my character.

I'm sorry, Lord, for the moments of selfishness when I worry about my convenience rather than doing what You want. Being convenient for myself is not being confident in You. I want to give my life to You as Jesus gave His life for me.

I can do this with strength from You. Thank You!

161

ACCOUNTABILITY

Confess your sins to each other and pray for each other so that you may be healed. The earnest prayer of a righteous person has great power and produces wonderful results.
JAMES 5:16 NLT

G od, thank You for letting me depend on You. There are some days when I feel like I must handle everything myself, but You tell me to lean on You. I'll rely on the power of prayer today and trust that You hear me and will act on my behalf. You tell me to encourage others to pray too.

Send me reliable and deep friendships with other followers. Give me the courage to be vulnerable with those in my life. You call me to pray for others and have them pray for me. I really want those connections, Lord.

I believe my prayers are powerful and affect my life. I know that when You hear my prayers, You act.

162

PROTECT YOUR PLANS

The LORD makes firm the steps of the one who
delights in him; though he may stumble, he will
not fall, for the LORD upholds him with his hand.
PSALM 37:23–24 NIV

God, thank You for being so steadfast. Once You establish a plan, nothing can get in its way. You are faithful and true; I can be confident in Your promises that my steps are directed by You, and I still seek Your face and follow Your ways.

Life can be unpredictable, and I can be unstable. I sometimes fall victim to my own selfishness and desires instead of counting on Your plans. Forgive me for those times.

Thank You, Father, that You never let me get in my own way. If my heart is on You and in the right place, You're still faithful even when I stumble. Like You did with King David, You protect Your children and Your plans.

163

RESURRECTING ME

And from Jesus Christ the faithful witness, the firstborn of the dead, and the ruler of kings on earth. To him who loves us and has freed us from our sins by his blood.
REVELATION 1:5 ESV

Jesus, thank You for dying on the cross for my sins. Thank You for being the absolute truth and a reliable source of all I need. I believe that after Your death, You were in the grave for only three days before You rose again, defeating darkness and ripping the veil between me and God.

Your resurrection means that all those who have accepted You as Savior will also have their own resurrection: the chance to be born again and after physical death to live in heaven.

I know, Lord, that You had to leave, but I'm confident You're coming back. You will return to reign in glory, and everyone will know Your name.

164

COURAGE LIKE PAUL'S

So take courage! For I believe God.
It will be just as he said.
ACTS 27:25 NLT

Father, I'm sorry when I let my emotions get the best of me. Circumstances can be overwhelming, and I sometimes let the littlest things disrupt my entire day. You can fill me with patience, bravery, joy, peace, and more. I want to be a light and a comfort to others around me, so I need You to fill me with all that is good.

I believe in You, God. I'm confident in Your message. At the end of the day, there's nothing else as true and constant. I'll not be ashamed of my faith or our relationship.

Paul told his friends these things too. I'll work daily for the faith and courage he had. When my friends need comfort or encouragement from me, give me the right words to say. I trust You'll know what they need.

165

WHEN I LIED

Truthful lips endure forever,
but a lying tongue lasts only a moment.
PROVERBS 12:19 NIV

*L*ord, I tell myself a little white lie isn't bad. But sometimes the lie after that one is bigger, and the one that follows becomes even larger. They build upon one another until I find myself living in a web of lies, trying to sort out the truth for myself. While it may work in the moment, all deceit is eventually revealed, no matter what the intention was.

Honesty is knowing that telling the truth is the right way for everyone even if it's hard. . .especially when it's hard.

Jesus is the embodiment of absolute truth, and though it may be harder to always be honest, I want to live every day like Your Son. Forgive me for the times I've lied. I promise to be better at telling the truth.

ACCORDING TO YOU

And Mary said, "Behold, I am the servant of the Lord; let it be to me according to your word." And the angel departed from her.
LUKE 1:38 ESV

Father, I know that You had a plan since the beginning, and when You presented Mary with Your will for her, she didn't say no. She didn't ask what would happen to her. She just replied she was a faithful servant and said it should be according to what You say.

I say the same thing to You today. I want Your will above mine. Open my eyes to what prevents me from putting total trust in You. I release my doubts and am ready to receive what You want for me.

Bless me with the courage of Mary, Lord, to do Your will, knowing that the plans are protected by You.

167

CONFIDENCE IN QUIET

This is what the Sovereign LORD, the Holy One of Israel,
says: "Only in returning to me and resting in me will
you be saved. In quietness and confidence is your
strength. But you would have none of it."
ISAIAH 30:15 NLT

Lord, when I need a rest, I don't go to You. I'm sorry. I turn away from You when I'm exhausted because I long to do Your work, and I don't want You to see me being weak. But You remind me that You love me in my weakness and want me to lean on You for strength.

There is confidence in quiet and confidence in waiting. Once my spirit is renewed, You will do amazing things just as You've done in my past. It hurts You when I hide. You want to help me in every aspect of my day. Starting now, when I feel exhausted, I'll turn to You for rest, relaxation, and complete renewal.

168

JESUS UNDERSTOOD

Jesus replied, "You do not realize now what I am doing, but later you will understand."
JOHN 13:7 NIV

Jesus, Your words have always been so full of meaning. While You directed this answer at Peter when You washed his feet, it meant so much more than just that simple act. You were also talking about the cross. Your disciples had no idea when they lived through the terrible days before and after Your sacrifice that it was Your plan the entire time to defeat death and conquer sin.

I may not understand why certain things happen, but I'm confident You're all-knowing. I have an advantage the disciples didn't have—I know the end of the story. I know You win! During trials, open my heart to learn, and give me the chance to grow into the woman You know I can be. I get to be someone who is courageous, kind, patient, and peaceful in Your name.

169

A PRAYER OF PSALM 23

*Your beauty and love chase after
me every day of my life.*
PSALM 23:6 MSG

Thank You, Father, that You look after me, that You guide and protect me through every circumstance. You lead me to absolute peace and renewal of my soul. You lead me down ways full of Your goodness.

Even though I face trials and hardships, I don't have to be afraid, because You're with me. Your Word and Your presence are protection and correction. They give me the comfort to be confident in myself.

You give me exactly what I need during hard times, and sometimes You even give me more than enough. Give me the peace to notice and enjoy the blessings You've given to me time and time again. Let my faith match those blessings.

I'm confident, God, that You'll be with me every day of my life. You'll never disappear. Even when my days in this life are over, I get to spend eternity with You.

170

DEATH DOESN'T WIN

"O death, where is your victory?
O death, where is your sting?"
1 CORINTHIANS 15:55 NLT

Thank You, Jesus, for triumphing over death and letting me share in that victory. Before this, death was the punishment for sin—the sting. But You endured that for all Your children and paid the price. You wiped away death for those who chose You.

I mourn for those who've gone before me, but I know that, while grieving lasts in the night, rejoicing comes in the morning. I can be joyful and confident that You already have the last word. I must do nothing but serve You as best I can, and one day I'll see my loved ones again and Your beautiful scars.

There is no captivity in this physical body, and I'm no longer chained to sin. You broke those bounds, and I'm free. Thank You!

CHOOSE GOODNESS

Finally, brothers and sisters, whatever is true,
whatever is noble, whatever is right, whatever is pure,
whatever is lovely, whatever is admirable—if anything
is excellent or praiseworthy—think about such things.
PHILIPPIANS 4:8 NIV

My thoughts can dictate my life, Lord. While they are only in my mind, they can sometimes affect my attitude and my actions. During these unsure times, I feel surrounded by negativity. People even ask me to complain, to dwell in annoyance, anger, or any other bad, icky feeling. I can't be confident in You if I'm focused only on negative things.

I know I have to fight back by pursuing the character of Jesus. I've always had the power to pick positivity over bitterness. Thank You, God, for being the best thing in my life. You constantly call me to try harder at choosing goodness. Even though it's harder, it is turning me into the best version of myself.

172

SUCH A TIME AS THIS

"If you keep quiet at a time like this, deliverance and relief for the Jews will arise from some other place, but you and your relatives will die. Who knows if perhaps you were made queen for just such a time as this?"
<small>ESTHER 4:14 NLT</small>

Lord, I know that You have brought me to this place for a reason. Let me know how to serve You, see You, and hear You. Remind me, God, that no one can stop Your plans. What You want done will get done, and I want to be a part of it. Please take away what is holding me back.

Thank You for this chance to make a difference in Your name. This could change lives as only You can! Thanks for the opportunity to show people who You are through me. You give me the strength to follow through. I will wait patiently for Your next instructions.

173

NO MATTER WHAT

Be cheerful no matter what; pray all the time;
thank God no matter what happens. This is the way
God wants you who belong to Christ Jesus to live.
1 Thessalonians 5:16–18 msg

God, teach me to be thankful and cheerful in every circumstance. Being both for all things—no matter what happens—means I trust You above all. Although the world around me is crumbling, I'm confident that You're in control. When I'm not thankful, show me why. What's standing in my way of proclaiming Your miracles and kindness? Help me deal with it, Lord.

I'll start counting my blessings daily no matter what the day holds. This way I can become used to seeing the good things in my life, building a firm foundation of joy, prayer, and thanksgiving. When a storm arrives, I will not be shaken. You created me to live this way, and Jesus died and rose again so I can continue to do so. Thank You.

174

FOR THE GOOD

"You intended to harm me, but God intended it for good to accomplish what is now being done, the saving of many lives."
GENESIS 50:20 NIV

Father, it's sometimes hard to imagine that not everyone is out for my good. Some may be jealous of what I have, our personalities just don't click, or they dislike me because of my relationship with You. This may cause them to do things that can really hurt me.

But Joseph and Jesus also experienced this. Although they were hated and betrayed, You turned their stories around. What was meant for their harm was ultimately used for Your good. Lord, thank You for constantly taking the painful parts of my past and present for the well-being of my future and the growth of the kingdom.

Not only does this benefit me, it helps others around me too. Give me confidence and peace as I trust what You're doing. Let others find You in me.

WHILE I'M HERE

Yet I am confident I will see the LORD's
goodness while I am here in the land of the living.
PSALM 27:13 NLT

*L*ord, thank You for the example we have of faith in the life of David. Even though David slayed a giant and was crowned king, He knew it was all by Your hand. He knew he still needed Your help. His psalms may come from a place of human weakness, but they totally acknowledge Your divine strength. When he performed terrible wrongs, You never abandoned David to his enemies. You protected him.

Thank You for doing the same with me. I want to fall to temptations and sin daily, but when I turn to You, I'm given the power to say no. I believe with my whole heart that You'll show Yourself in amazing ways while I'm here in this life. All I have to do is open my eyes and soul to see.

TRANSFORMED BY FAITH

*By faith Rahab the prostitute did not perish
with those who were disobedient, because she
had given a friendly welcome to the spies.*
HEBREWS 11:31 ESV

God, Rahab was a woman who was looked down upon during her time in history. She was a known prostitute and a liar. But You, Father, don't remember her as such. She may have had a shadowed past, but she was then recorded to have great faith. Despite her sins, by her faith and Your grace, she was redeemed and added to the lineage of Christ. She is a wonderful example of character being transformed by faith. I know I can be one too.

Lord, I feel like Rahab some days. Burdened by my past but also believing You in a land that doesn't. So many have turned from the Gospel and ask me to do the same. Let me be transformed by my faith. Allow me to stand strong in Jesus when others choose differently. I'll forever choose You.

177

THE HOLY SPIRIT

This is how we know that we live in him
and he in us: He has given us of his Spirit.
1 JOHN 4:13 NIV

*L*ord, thank You so much for the Holy Spirit. Thank You that the Spirit is how You live in me, how You teach me the character of Jesus. This helps me pray and gives me strength to overcome sin. This is also how You comfort and heal my brokenness.

God, let me feel the Holy Spirit more deeply than I ever have before. I'm sorry for sometimes forgetting about this beautiful gift You've given me. I know You're always present, but I invite the Spirit into a more active role in my life today. I want to walk hand in hand with You, Father. Thank You for blessing me with the small taste of what eternity will be like.

178

LIKE IT IS DONE

The people who walk in darkness will see a
great light. For those who live in a land
of deep darkness, a light will shine.
ISAIAH 9:2 NLT

Thank You, God, that the moment this world slipped into sin, You had a plan to redeem it. The day I was born, You created a path for me to You and my calling. If my heart is fully directed to what's important, sin can't get in my way even when I stumble. Jesus made sure of it.

Let my language be like the prophets' in the Bible. They spoke as if what they predicated had already come to pass. Give me the confidence to act like what You promise is already done. That is true faith!

I may have been held captive by sin, but I was freed by Christ. It's time for me to start living like it.

179

I'M GOD'S HEIR

So you are no longer a slave, but a son,
and if a son, then an heir through God.
GALATIANS 4:7 ESV

*L*ord, when I look at the rest of creation, I realize how small I am. I know to the world I'm just a face in the crowd, a number, overwhelmingly insignificant. But You see me. You care. I was made in Your image, and You knew me before I was even conceived. Thank You, God.

Once I accept Jesus into my life, I'm no longer a slave to this world or sin, and I get to step into my rightful place as Your child. Help me take that step. Let me lay aside what's holding me back.

If I'm Your daughter, I'm an heir. I'm protected and loved. While I feel out of place in so many aspects of my life, I can be fully at home in Your presence.

180

EVERYTHING'S NEW

And the one sitting on the throne said, "Look, I am making everything new!" And then he said to me, "Write this down, for what I tell you is trustworthy and true." And he also said, "It is finished! I am the Alpha and the Omega—the Beginning and the End. To all who are thirsty I will give freely from the springs of the water of life."
REVELATION 21:5–6 NLT

✺

Thank You, Father, that You make all things new. Thank You for always being the Source of truth and life. I never have to worry about saving my own life because the debt was paid and the deal was finished on the cross. You're in the beginning of every journey in life and standing at the finish line with open arms, welcoming me home. But most importantly, You walk beside me, carrying or dragging me when needed.

Thank You for each new morning, each day, each night. Each new moment, I will confidently praise Your name.

SCRIPTURE INDEX

OLD TESTAMENT

NEW TESTAMENT

ABOUT THE AUTHOR

Ellie Zumbach is a freelance writer and actor in northeastern Ohio. She earned a BA in Creative Writing from Malone University in Canton, Ohio. Her writings have been awarded the Malone Writers Prize in areas of Fiction, Creative Nonfiction, and Poetry, and presented at Taylor University's Making Literature Conference in 2017 and 2019. She has been published in *The Cobalt Review*, *Bella Grace*, and is a current contributor to *Memoirs of a Virtuous Woman*, an online devotional site for women. She has always believed that stories are some of the most important things in the world and spent her years growing up on a small dairy farm reading as many as she could.

Looking for More Encouragement for Your Heart?

Worry Less, Pray More

This purposeful devotional guide features 180 readings and prayers designed to help alleviate your worries as you learn to live in the peace of the Almighty God, who offers calm for your anxiety-filled soul.

Paperback / 978-1-68322-861-5 / $4.99

Too Blessed to Be Stressed: 3-Minute Devotions for Women

You'll find the spiritual pick-me-up you need in *Too Blessed to Be Stressed: 3-Minute Devotions for Women*—180 uplifting readings from bestselling author Debora M. Coty pack a power-ful dose of inspiration, encouragement, humor, and faith into just-right-sized readings for your busy schedule.

Paperback / 978-1-63409-569-3 / $4.99